RTI

**FROM
ALL
SIDES**

*W*e are at a crossroads.

We can either use response to intervention

as an opportunity

to rebuild a positive climate

or allow it to devolve into something

that takes us even farther

from the reason most of us

became teachers.

foreword by Linda Hoyt

Mary Howard

RTI FROM ALL SIDES

What Every Teacher *Needs* to Know

WHEN TO STEP BACK

WHEN TO PROCEED WITH CAUTION

WHEN TO MOVE FORWARD

HEINEMANN
Portsmouth, NH

Heinemann
361 Hanover Street
Portsmouth, NH 03801–3912
www.heinemann.com

Offices and agents throughout the world

Library of Congress Cataloging-in-Publication Data
Howard, Mary
    RTI from all sides : what every teacher needs to know / Mary Howard.
        p. cm.
    Includes bibliographical references and index.
    ISBN-13: 978-0-325-02670-1
    ISBN-10: 0-325-02670-X
    1. Problem children—Education—United States.   2. Behavior disorders in children—United States.   3. Learning disabled children—Education—United States. I. Title.
LC4802.H68 2009
371.93—dc22   2008055801

Editor: Wendy Murray
Production: Lynne Costa
Cover and interior designs: Lisa Fowler
Typesetter: House of Equations, Inc.
Manufacturing: Louise Richardson

Printed in the United States of America on acid-free paper
13   12   11   10   09   VP   4   5

*This book is dedicated to the loving
memory of my mother and father,
Jim and Sue Howard.
Every child's gift would shine brightly
if only they could have the same loving support
that was my birthright.*

CONTENTS

FOREWORD

Most of us became educators because of a deep passion for learning, for challenging and supporting children as they reach to maximize their own potential. The legislation that launched Response to Intervention (RTI) is designed with that same focus. Its purpose is to reduce the number of learners referred to learning disabilities or special education programs by providing intensive and effective instruction before children begin to fail. It appropriately places emphasis on the importance of early and effective teaching and learning for *all students* by amplifying the role of excellent instruction. However, to ensure that RTI maintains a focus on the students it strives to serve, we must be aware that danger lurks below the surface . . .

There has been a mad rush in the publishing world to produce "products and programs" for RTI. Well-meaning educators, wishing to live up to the challenges of RTI, are launching initiatives before really studying the legislation and developing the instructional frameworks that are needed. The result: Some of the very programs that improved word calling and did little for comprehension in Reading First are being replicated by publishers—under the umbrella of RTI!

In this powerful book that sizzles with commitment to teachers as thoughtful professionals, Mary Howard holds up her hand and reminds us to "Slow down!" Slow down enough to engage in the reflective thinking from which great instruction is born. She invites us to be bold enough to be honest about what we are and are not doing to support individuals in daily instruction, to ask questions, and have ongoing, honest conversations as a schoolwide staff. Mary wisely reminds us that because RTI is significant and important, this is not the time to play it safe and remain passive. It is time to stand strong and defend what's good for kids—in spite of products and programs—in spite of recent trends.

Throughout, Mary makes it clear that she is first and foremost a teacher. Her experience and her heart reside in the classroom and it shows on every page of this book. Mary reminds us that targeted instruction, as described in RTI, is designed to teach struggling readers the same strategies used by proficient readers. She reminds us that kids need texts and tasks at appropriate levels every day. She reminds us that meaningful, high-interest resources and active student engagement are essential elements of quality instruction. She champions the responsive teachers who utilize formative, ongoing assessments and develop instruction to match. She firmly but kindly turns our attention to the fact that small groups working with "just right texts" and one-to-one coaching are the cornerstones of quality instruction . . . as well as the cornerstones of quality interventions in the RTI tiers.

In a salute to classroom teachers, Mary states

> You—and you alone—are the ringmaster who will make a difference for readers who struggle. What you do matters when you make every day matter for your students. You add the talented human touch we are dangerously close to losing.

This book is desperately needed in districts and state departments everywhere. It is loaded with the "here's how" of interventions that are right for kids and right for the educators who serve them. It profiles RTI as a framework for increasing intentional instruction, making the wisest possible teaching moves with the neediest students—and keeping the emphasis on knowledgeable educators rather than "programs."

If this book could become a prerequisite to implementation, I fully believe that the goals of RTI may well be realized.

—Linda Hoyt

ACKNOWLEDGMENTS

My journey as a fledgling writer has been an exciting and fulfilling one. This book is a culmination of almost four decades of joyful learning alongside dedicated colleagues and wonderful children who have deepened my understanding of expert literacy teaching. My devotion to children and teaching gave me just the stimulus I needed to take this giant step down a new path.

I have learned that a book happens with the hard work and dedication of many people. First and foremost, I am grateful to have been placed in the capable and talented hands of Wendy Murray—editor extraordinaire. Her expertise and willingness to listen to the questions and fears of a novice writer turned a dream into a reality. She knew just the right phrasing to express my ideas, and her generosity and support throughout this remarkable process have been paramount. I am also grateful to Judy Wallis for sharing her knowledge and expert writing suggestions. Their combined advice has made it possible to accomplish far more than I could have done alone.

I am indebted to Lisa Fowler, who created a book cover beyond my wildest dreams. Thank you for a picture that says one thousand words and reflects my thoughts, hopes, and ideas about RTI in a single beautiful design.

Good friends have been important to this process in so many ways. Special thanks to Linda Holliman and Susan Fitzell for reading my first draft and offering feedback and encouragement. I appreciate the suggestions of experienced writer and friend Colleen Politano. Love and appreciation also goes to Joy Paquin, the angel sitting on my shoulder. Thank you to my friends Joan Knight, Boyce Heidenreich, and Ken Young for their encouragement. I am especially grateful to Linda Hoyt for never wavering in her belief that a writer existed inside of me. Thank you for encouraging me to give that writer a voice.

So many talented writers contributed to my literacy understandings—Regie Routman, Debbie Miller, Linda Hoyt, Sharon Taberski, and too many others to list. Marie Clay taught me much about the literacy process and inspired a sense of curiosity that has strengthened over time. A special thank-you to my doctoral advisor, Dr. Kouider Mokhtari, for allowing me to explore this curiosity with his expert support. I am particularly indebted to the tireless work of Dr. Richard Allington. He taught me that we cannot simply sit back and hope for change—we must be the impetus. I admire his willingness to "go against the grain" even when it's not the easy path. His courage has emboldened me to make assertions that I know will ruffle feathers.

Thank you to the dedicated teachers of Lincoln Elementary School in Lawton, Oklahoma. For the past four years, they have honored me with the opportunity to support their growth toward literacy excellence. I am extremely proud of their accomplishments, including recent designation as National Title 1 Distinguished School of 2008–2009. The talented leadership of Robbie Gillis, Kim Erwin, and Vicki Turner has allowed the world to see what I saw four years ago—a shining example of literacy and learning. I am also grateful to the wonderful teachers and school leaders of Bishop Elementary School and Swinney Elementary School in Lawton, Oklahoma. I have learned so much from these talented teachers and school leaders who allow me to learn with and through them.

I am so blessed to have a loving family. My brothers, Jim, John, and Mike, have always been ardent supporters. I am eternally grateful to my sister Sandy—my best friend, advisor, confidante, and encourager. Thank you for never complaining about the months away from home or with my head hovered over a computer and for lifting my spirits when my confidence waned. I am especially grateful for Cyndi, Kristin, and Tracey. They make me the proudest "second mother" and have blessed me with the most amazing nieces and nephews. Dan, Jude, Moses, Simon, Julian, Kendall, Carlee, Madeline, and Codie added to a growing circle my brothers started with Brittyn, Barrett, Austin, Dan, Elliot, Rick, and Rachel.

Finally, I am indebted to the many children who have enriched my life in nearly four decades of teaching. They are my most important reading teachers, stimulating new thinking that has opened the door to a growing understanding of literacy. Collectively, they were the catalyst for this book. I am honored to be a teacher, a title I will continue to wear proudly.

INTRODUCTION

*A*fter a heated discussion about response to intervention (RTI) with a colleague, my friend placed a scrap of paper in my hand and said, "Mary, you have to write a book and say those things to teachers." I looked down in terror at the scribbled name and phone number of a Heinemann editor. Could I contribute anything to the topic? What would my angle be?

It didn't take me long to realize that my angle was to add an *s* to *angle* because, as I had told my friend that day, RTI is multi-faceted, and if we don't slow down and look at it from several angles, we risk potentially flawed interpretations of it careening into our schools. I wrote this book so teachers would have a guide to help them make good decisions for themselves, their students, and their schools as we move from RTI in theory and in the marketplace to RTI implemented in *real* classrooms with *real* students.

What got me involved in RTI? The 2004 reauthorization of the Individuals with Disabilities Education Improvement Act (IDEA) led to the creation and rapid growth of the general education initiative now referred to as *response to intervention*. Given my career as a literacy consultant and coach, RTI immediately sparked my interest. Having devoted nearly four decades to better understanding how to meet the needs of struggling readers, I was excited by an initiative that could make schoolwide differentiated instruction a priority. RTI's emphasis on the classroom teacher as the first line of defense in this process seemed smart. If RTI can be the tipping point for schools, defining and rallying around expert classroom instruction above all—well, count me in.

I set out on a quest to learn more that involved hours of study in schools, professional reading, and discussions with teachers and administrators. The more I learned, the more I believed RTI could be the safety net needed to catch struggling readers *before* they falter and get stuck in an endless game of catch-up. Clearly, the status quo for helping struggling readers wasn't working.

As this book goes to press, RTI is in what I call its "potential phase," meaning it's too early to tell how it will shake out. It has the *potential* for making effective, excellent literacy instruction a collaborative venture in our schools. It has the potential to:

- Place heavy emphasis on early intervention
- Rally every member of the school staff around a common cause
- Be a catalyst for ongoing professional development
- Help teachers define and sustain research-based best instructional practices in literacy teaching
- Generate high-quality ongoing assessments to inform instruction
- Promote interventions for struggling readers that are targeted to individual need
- Initiate instructional support at increasing levels of intensity
- Remove existing barriers between instructional support systems

Consider these bulleted points my first "green light" to you. As the cover of this book signals, my goal is to offer teachers information that will help them know what aspects of RTI to green-light immediately, with confidence that they are good for kids, and what aspects warrant "yellow" and even "red light" cautious responses. So here's a first yellow light to consider:

Beware of RTI's rapid commercialization and rigid interpretation by well-meaning but sometimes misinformed stakeholders—whoever they may be. In many schools I've visited, the implementation of RTI is having the opposite of the intended effect of helping readers, because scripted programs purchased in the name of RTI are entirely sidelining effective literacy practices. In other scenarios I've seen, RTI initiatives do not show teachers and other professionals how to successfully execute the instructional piece of RTI. Still worse, teachers' decision-making power with regard to their readers—their day-to-day professional judgment—is in some cases being systematically taken away. In their effort to comply with RTI mandates, many schools move students from one adult to another for intervention, leaving the child to synthesize all the information. Often these adults have little contact with one another, generally because RTI has been hurriedly put into place without ongoing professional support, and so teachers flounder. In many schools, administrators are plugging separate and distinct programs into each tier of intervention, giving teachers little hope of coordination.

We cannot continue business as usual, taking what hasn't worked and renaming it RTI. In a recent *Education Week* article, "Federal Path for Reading

Questioned," Kathleen Kennedy Manzo (2008) points out: "One of the largest and most rigorous studies ever undertaken by the U.S. Department of Education found that the $6 billion funding for Reading First has helped more students 'crack the code' to identify letters and words, but it has not had an effect on reading comprehension among 1st, 2nd, and 3rd graders in participating schools" (1).

The article goes on to point out that even with a study of this scale, little or nothing can be gleaned from it about *how* to improve comprehension. I mention this article for a couple of reasons. One, because so much is still murky about Reading First, you better believe that its failed practices will morph into RTI initiatives by the sheer force of politics and people in power who are invested in them. And two, the article reminds us that you can spend *six billion* dollars on Reading First, RTI, or anything you want, but if the framework is not well designed and implemented, and rooted in practical, research-based pedagogy, it won't get our young readers where they need to go.

First and foremost, this book is written for the educators who work tirelessly to ensure that RTI maintains a focus on the students it strives to serve. Researchers, authors, consultants, and seminar leaders can only lay the foundation for RTI; those who work directly with students ultimately hold the key to its future success.

I am not a researcher. I am not a university professor. I am not a program developer. I am a teacher who cares deeply about children and teachers. I am committed to children who struggle and the teachers who work so diligently to support them, and to anyone in the "business" of education who puts children's needs first. Which reminds me—I must call my friend and thank her for that crumpled piece of paper.

CHAPTER 1

The Paths Leading to the RTI Crossroads

*M*y green thumb came only as a result of the mistakes I made
while learning to see things from the plant's point of view.

—*H. Fred Hale*

It's a hot August morning in Stella, Missouri, 1972. The classroom is straight
from the set of *Little House on the Prairie*—flowered curtains, colorful wall dec-
orations, old-fashioned lift-top tables with chairs, books filling every open
nook. It's my first day as a new teacher, a wide-eyed, idealistic twenty-two-year-
old, standing in the doorway waiting impatiently for my students to arrive.

Because I am a special education teacher, I have been assigned a small,
freestanding building apart from the main campus. Not yet daunted by the isolation, I give each child who walks through my door a welcoming smile. These
twelve students, ages six to fourteen, represent almost every area of special
need I have studied over the past four years.

Before an hour has passed, my confidence starts to fade as I realize that my
university courses have failed me. I had been promised clearly defined roles:

I was the teacher; they were the students. I would teach my students everything I knew, and they would learn my sage lessons eagerly. I feel the promise slowly dwindle as the day wears on. In a single day, I learn the first of many life lessons from twelve students with unique needs, as *they* become *my* teachers. They teach me what they need, and it's all different. I know I have as much to learn from them as they will learn from me.

During the next thirty-seven years of ever-shifting educational trends, my understanding of the blurred roles of teacher and student will deepen. I'll take it in stride as I become a more responsive teacher and trust the continuous tango between teaching and learning. Gradually, I become a better teacher equipped to make good decisions for my students. I learn to refute the education field's false promises and foolishness and to develop an internal radar for spotting new ideas and research worth integrating into my existing repertoire. The sense of empowerment I share with my colleagues during these years comes from our central role in instructional decision making. This engagement feeds our careers and makes us even more responsive to our students.

Fast-forward to 2008. On an April morning I stand before one hundred teachers to give a presentation on response to intervention. Looking around the room, I don't see wide-eyed idealism in their expressions. Instead, I see teachers anxiously waiting, pens poised, for *the* answers to their questions. "Tell me what to do," their faces seem to say. I stand before them, displaying my colorful PowerPoint slides, and a feeling of loss comes over me. I'm a million miles from the schoolroom where I came into my own as a teacher. The sense of optimism I savored then seems impossible now, to both experienced teachers who relinquish more autonomy with each passing year and those new to the profession who never tasted it.

What happened? These teachers are quaking in their boots from the pressures bombarding them. They've lost their sense of direction. As I begin my presentation, each teacher leans forward and begins writing down almost every word I say.

After my talk, my thoughts turn to the state of education today and how dramatically our lives have changed in such a short time. In the last decade, dedicated teachers have watched with sadness as a testing culture has put a stranglehold on education. As a result, many teachers spend far too much of the day following a package, mandate, or script and far too little of it making enthusiastic professional decisions. The energy devoted to raising test scores has left little room for the knowledgeable collaboration that can guide what both research and experience confirm will have the greatest impact on learning.

We are at a crossroads. We can either use response to intervention as an opportunity to rebuild a positive climate or allow it to devolve into something that takes us even further from the reason most of us became teachers.

In the last decade, dedicated teachers have watched with sadness as a testing culture has put a stranglehold on education.

The Promise of RTI: Solid Research Underpinnings

Response to intervention is a multitiered approach to early intervention for struggling readers, initially focused on K–2, but gradually extending to all grade levels. The overarching idea behind RTI is targeted instruction to expertly match each student's needs. By intervening and supporting struggling students early, we can get most kids to read at grade level within the regular classroom, tier 1. More intense instruction is given to those who need second- and third-tier interventions to accelerate their learning and enable them to catch up to the proficient readers in their class. Put simply, if it works, these kids can avoid special education.

RTI is a relatively new term in education, but the ideals inherent in RTI were highlighted in 1995 when Richard Allington and Sean Walmsley published the edited collection *No Quick Fix: Rethinking Literacy Programs in America's Elementary Schools*. The book cautioned against fragmentation of support services and advocated proven support models for struggling readers and the concept of a tiered approach to teaching and intervention. It emphasized the need for an instructional framework, intervention, ongoing assessment, and multimethod and multilevel instruction.

In the 2007 revision, *No Quick Fix: The RTI Edition*, the editors describe RTI as "old wine with a new label." Given that the groundbreaking models for intervention are still widely accepted today, this seems apt. John Pikulski, former president of the International Reading Association (IRA), called the book a "launching pad" for RTI (2007). Perhaps if we'd heeded cautions the authors originally laid down about fragmentation and their call for high-quality instruction and interventions, I would feel more surefooted about the nation's move toward RTI. I worry that we won't take the time to learn from past lessons and failures in special education initiatives and define for ourselves why they failed and what was missing—and that, as a result, RTI may join the ranks of one more good idea gone awry. The most recent Reading First report (November 2008), which summarizes its failures to make statistically significant, positive changes in reading performance, should serve as a timely warning to those implementing RTI so that we do not repeat the past. As teachers, we must force ourselves to avoid passivity and compliance, and insist that we be in the driver's seat. We will do right by our struggling readers and help them achieve only if we collaborate to get this one right.

Let's look on the bright side: We have a solid understanding of what effective literacy instruction looks like and what teachers can do to make it happen (Allington and Johnston 2000; Allington 2002; Taylor et al. 2002; Allington 2009).

We have a solid understanding of what effective literacy instruction looks like and what teachers can do to make it happen.

These studies reveal over and over again the ways in which exemplary teachers plan and teach. We need to build on this knowledge and amplify the role of excellent instruction as we implement RTI. We should not allow RTI to be framed as yet another *new* vision of literacy—by publishers, government, or well-intentioned administrators who may be feeling the pressure to "fix it" quickly. Before we consider using any RTI resource in our schools, we need to evaluate it in light of what we know about effective literacy instruction and its past success in producing performance gains for students.

NCLB: One Catalyst for RTI

RTI is a hot topic now, largely because it's an outgrowth of the No Child Left Behind Act (NCLB) of 2000. In 1997, Congress formed the fourteen-member National Reading Panel (NRP). These people were assigned the daunting task of analyzing the existing research about how children learn to read and the factors that contribute to literacy development. The breadth of their task forced the panel to narrow their review of the research. The NRP report, published in 2000, did confirm long-standing beliefs such as the role of early intervention and parent support, and it extended our understanding of reading instruction.

Two key concepts that were heavily emphasized in the NRP report were incorporated into both NCLB and the RTI initiative: (1) The need for research-based instruction and (2) the five components or pillars of effective literacy (phonemic awareness, phonics, fluency, vocabulary, comprehension). And wouldn't you know it, all five components rapidly appeared on the annual What's Hot? list in *Reading Today* (Cassidy and Cassidy),[1] although their inclusion has since declined. Phonemic awareness fell off the hot list in 2007, followed by phonics in 2008. In 2008, fluency lost ground as what "should be hot" while comprehension and vocabulary held fast. This shift likely suggests that educators realized the pillars were unequal in their importance. While phonemic awareness and phonics are necessary in learning to read, they are insufficient to make a reader who understands and enjoys reading. Yet the influence of the NRP report on RTI endures. One must wonder why the "big five" rise and fall like hemlines. What does it say about our field that one minute these "pillars" are all essential, and the next some are dispensable?

A rapid outpouring of publications followed the NRP report (publishers pay attention to what's "hot"), and I'm not suggesting they all deserve caution. In

---

[1] Each year since 1996, twenty-five literacy leaders have ranked topics in *Reading Today* as *hot* or *not hot* based on the attention they receive. (Two categories—*what should be hot* and *what should not be hot*—were added in 2002.)

fact, there are a handful of solid professional books—an excellent recent one is *What Really Matters in Response to Intervention* by Richard Allington (2009)—and some highly useful websites, such as What Works Clearinghouse (http://ies.ed.gov/ncee/wwc/) and RTI Action Network (www.rtinetwork.org/). These publications and the increased popularity of RTI have also led to a deluge of programs. I can't help but see flashing red lights over some of the products on the market. Many of them raise concerns that warrant attention:

- ***Programs that position the five pillars as equal and exclusive.*** Any program on the market that suggests equal attention to the five pillars set forth in the NRP report, and doesn't go beyond these five components, needs to be looked at with great caution.

- ***Programs that consistently teach one component in isolation.*** I'd also look carefully at any product that promotes a pillar in *isolation* rather than within the broader base of meaningful reading. For example, fluency is often reduced to a matter of reading speed or blown out of proportion to support a higher-priced product rather than good pedagogy. Products often promote fluency as the *end* rather that the *means* to proficient reading and understanding.

- ***Programs that emphasize teaching phonics in isolation.*** Any program that focuses exclusively on phonics outside the context of reading high-quality texts is also suspect. Readers must orchestrate many skills in becoming successful readers, and while certain aspects might be isolated in teaching, sound instruction views text-based readers as the goal.

- ***Programs with questionable research support.*** Many popular RTI programs reflect little research support. Reading Recovery is the only intervention program to be awarded the highest success ranking by the U.S. Department of Education Institute of Education Sciences What Works Clearinghouse (http://ies.ed.gov/ncee/wwc/), yet few schools turn to it for an intervention template. As a trained Reading Recovery teacher, I have found its focus on varied instructional strategies that follow children and their needs, rather than a rigid series of steps, to be powerfully effective. Schools must determine whether the programs they are using have sufficient research as well as a track record of proven success to back up their related lessons and frameworks.

- ***Programs considered effective based on popularity rather than research.*** It is particularly disconcerting that the most popular reading programs fail to meet the panel's criteria for being research based. They weren't published in a peer-reviewed journal and have not received the rigorous scientific study required by the panel. Moreover, they are rarely subjected to the fine-toothed inspection applied to teachers. Interestingly, some programs published in the name of RTI have received low scores from What Works Clearinghouse.[2] I can't think of a better way to annihilate RTI. Too much energy is expended searching for "program nirvana" and too little exploring the high-quality instruction good teachers provide, with and without resources.

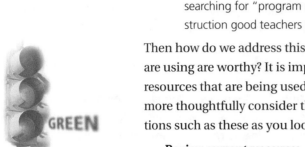

GREEN

Then how do we address this red light issue and ensure that the programs we are using are worthy? It is imperative that schools take a long hard look at the resources that are being used so that adjustments can be made and we can more thoughtfully consider those that may be secured in the future. Ask questions such as these as you look at current and potential resources.

Review current resources

- Is it working?
- How are the students faring?
- How do we know it is effective?
- How might we adjust it?
- Is flexibility encouraged?
- Are leveled text resources available and of high quality?
- Is there a limit of "stuff" and focus on active engagement?
- Is teacher judgment valued?
- What resources can we bring in to make it more effective?
- Does it have a proven track record?

Review potential resources

- Will it work in our particular school?
- If it appears on a list of "research-blessed" programs, is the research really solid?
- What adjustments will be needed to enhance these resources?
- What supportive scaffolds will ensure success within and beyond each grade level?
- Does the program emphasize varied instructional contexts, including teacher demonstrations, guided practice, and independent application?
- Is the focus on effective teaching practices or on overscripted, narrow instruction?
- Can interventions be used across tiers?

---

[2] What Works Clearinghouse—http://ies.ed.gov/ncee/wwc—evaluates programs for evidence of success in alphabetics (phonemic awareness, phonological awareness, letter recognition, print awareness, and phonics), reading fluency, comprehension (vocabulary and reading comprehension), and general reading achievement.

- Does the program encourage integrating what we know about excellent reading instruction?
- On what research does the program stand?

Evaluating the effectiveness of any program is an ongoing process as the needs of students change. The principal, curriculum specialist, and all literacy leaders are part of this process as we make a commitment to quality instruction and thoughtfully planned resources. The effectiveness of our instructional practices *are* impacted by the resources we use, so this is an important, continuing goal. RTI cannot simply become an excuse to purchase a program that is labeled RTI but does not represent the quality that is needed to meet our students' needs. And once we make these choices, we must insist on maintaining a key role in their selection and use and opt for the most effective programs possible.

What Do We Mean by Scientifically Based Research?

The concept of *scientific research–based instruction* is inherent in NCLB and RTI. While terminology varies (*scientifically based, research-based, evidence-based, scientific evidence–based*), the meaning is essentially the same—instruction that has a strong basis in research. Selecting instruction that has a greater likelihood of working is certainly professionally responsible. In fact, we need to make sure more of our instruction is supported by evidence. But here's the rub: the term is sometimes used sloppily to support a program or practice that is not in fact backed by sound, replicable research. In other cases the term may be given *too* much weight by those serving up mandates, creating a climate in which anything that hasn't been "tested scientifically" is therefore questionable practice. (Independent reading time in school suffered this fate, but more about that later.)

In the wake of the NRP report, exemplary teachers, researchers, and thinkers were alarmed that instructional practices we know from *our* research are effective were virtually ignored. In response, the NRP admitted that it was not possible for a panel of volunteers to examine critically this entire body of research literature. In fact this resulted in some programs being labeled "scientifically based" when they were not.

The panel's exclusive focus on experimental and quasi-experimental research led them to ignore a wealth of research, as they excluded Durkin, Hart and Riseley, and even Piaget (Tooms, Padak, and Rasinski 2007). That this research didn't warrant a blip on the panel's radar screen ignited debate and, I daresay, divisiveness that continues to this day. What's interesting is that as this book goes to press, I detect that good old pendulum beginning to swing again. New data on the failure of NCLB, a new administration in Washington, and a weak economy raise new and old questions. Mark my words: independent reading with guidance and feedback, trade books, and literature circle discussions are going to earn their rightful place at the table again. But we aren't there yet. We are still living in the shadow of NCLB, and for some teachers new to the profession, a diminished view of literacy and instructional possibilities is all they've known.

Lessons Learned from the Five Literacy Pillars

Because the five pillars have become the benchmark against which good programs and good teachers are measured, teachers and schools need to reexamine these five components of literacy emphasized in the panel's report. Therefore, I'll spend some time with them here to build a common understanding of these aspects of literacy and, hopefully, provide a filter so that RTI in your school isn't built on misconceptions.

 YELLOW

Specifically, we need to be clear that these five components are not necessarily the most important aspects of literacy, and they are not equally weighted in terms of relevance. For example, phonemic awareness and fluency are rightfully important in first grade, but what percentage of students needs direct instruction in these areas in third grade? And what aspects of literacy, such as motivation and critical literacy, are suspiciously offstage? The panel openly admitted that they didn't address many worthwhile topics and practices because there simply wasn't time. Once again, time constraints narrowed the frame that would allow us to view literacy from a broader perspective.

The brief overview of each pillar below is followed by a dose of classroom reality.

Phonemic Awareness

THE PANEL Phonemes are the smallest units of sound in spoken language—forty-one sounds form syllables and words in the English language. Phonemic awareness is an ability to recognize and manipulate spoken words by blending, deleting, and substituting these sounds. Most children develop this skill when they are very young, often before starting school. Systematic or explicit instruction using one or two phonemes at a time is most effective. Fourteen to eighteen hours of phonemic awareness training is recommended during an academic year, or fifteen minutes a day. It is only *one* part of a total reading program, and no single method appears more effective than another. Instruction based on language, songs, and games is most effective, and small-group activities produce greater gains than a whole-group focus.

THE REALITY   Phonemic awareness training has become a mainstay of many early literacy programs that extend well beyond fifteen minutes a day and supersede real literacy experiences. This is especially problematic for the many students who enter school with this knowledge in place and are ready for reading instruction. While some children may need more explicit forms of phonemic awareness training, most develop this understanding with language play, in the context of rhyming texts and songs (Opitz 2000). Unfortunately, an approach that emphasizes simple, brief, and enjoyable activities is not evident in most classrooms, where too much time is spent on isolated, repetitive drills fueled by the letter-a-week mentality.

Phonics

THE PANEL   Phonics is letter-to-sound correspondence, or the ability to match sounds to letters in reading and spelling. Phonics is an important skill that should be taught early. Phonics instruction should be both systematic (intentional) and incidental (opportunistic) and can be *synthetic*, or explicit (letter by letter), or *analytic* (whole words and patterns). Moving as quickly as possible to an *analytic* approach ensures that readers will see "chunks" in words. This is particularly important as readers encounter longer and more complex words. A systematic, explicit approach using specific, sequential phonics elements is recommended. Teachers are cautioned, however, not to let phonics become the dominant program, but rather to ensure that students can apply phonetic concepts in meaningful and authentic activities.

THE REALITY   Phonics in isolation has gradually become the key feature of instruction, often with little opportunity to *use* phonics by applying it to the reading of interesting texts. Little research supports decodable texts, yet struggling readers are subjected to stories that place priority on sound sequences over meaning. Many new intervention programs created with RTI in mind come with little books telling senseless stories, often suggesting to young readers that meaning doesn't matter. Phonics-first proponents prevail with instruction that focuses on synthetic, over analytic phonics despite a lack of evidence showing it is more effective. I regularly hear the painful sound of *bu-bu-bu, cu-cu-cu, du-du-du* ringing through hallways as children agonizingly huff and puff at print in lieu of reading real words in interesting stories. These approaches give struggling readers little reason to view reading as a quest worthy of the effort.

Fluency

THE PANEL   Oral reading fluency is an essential component of proficient reading. It includes the ability to read orally with accuracy, speed, and expression using prosodic features such as intonation, phrasing, pace, pausing, and inflection. Students develop fluency from ample practice reading meaningful texts with support. In fact, students who read slightly below the level of core reading programs may *appear* disfluent when the text difficulty is actually the problem. Research demonstrates that independent reading without guidance and feedback has no positive effect on fluency. Findings do show that repeated oral reading practice *with* teacher feedback is effective, particularly with challenging materials.

THE REALITY   The panel's recommendation of repeated reading of challenging texts suggests that whole-group oral reading is justified. Fluency in isolation has become increasingly prevalent even though most children develop fluency within higher focus of comprehension. Although the panel emphasized that round robin reading is ineffective, it's used regularly across grades. Too often, teachers view fluency solely as a matter of speed rather than meaning making. Oral reading has taken the place of silent reading even in the intermediate grades. This is problematic for older struggling readers. Worse, the panel's statement regarding independent silent reading has led many schools to abandon self-selected independent reading altogether. Sadly, some schools have literally outlawed silent reading despite significant research supporting it (see Krashen 2004; Allington 2009; Atwell 2007—none of which met the panel's research criteria).

Vocabulary

THE PANEL   Knowing word meanings has a strong impact on the reader's ability to comprehend. Vocabulary refers to knowledge of spoken *and* written words, both equally important. Words are easier to learn in print after students have been exposed to them orally. Findings show that vocabulary should be developed both explicitly (direct instruction) and incidentally (authentic experiences). Instructional methods that provide repeated exposure to words in a wide variety of contexts and in ways that actively engage students are likely to increase vocabulary. Teachers are encouraged to talk about words in varied experiences throughout the school day.

THE REALITY   Certainly vocabulary is linked to proficient reading—the more words students know and understand, the more meaningful the reading. Therefore, the more access students have to appropriate and interesting reading material, the more likely their vocabulary will grow. Unfortunately, many programs emphasize quantity over quality, prescribe questionable passive activities, and provide little opportunity for repeated exposure of texts that is so critical. In fact, the same key vocabulary words are often emphasized in texts at, below, and above grade level. The texts read are therefore often less interesting, and the words become more important than the stories. There is no limit to word drills and worksheets, and the ineffective practice of copying words and definitions from the dictionary continues. Depth of knowledge is replaced by surface word study. Words in isolation are emphasized over words in the context of meaningful and interesting stories. Emphasizing key vocabulary is important but passive strategies for learning words is an ineffective way to accomplish this.

Comprehension

THE PANEL   *Comprehension* refers to the reader's ability to understand and interpret a text. It is a complex, active process of making meaning that requires a wide range of skills and strategies. *Comprehension strategies* are intentional actions that increase our ability to understand, remember, and use textual information. Proficient readers monitor meaning by selecting cognitive strategies that support understanding or use specific strategies when meaning breaks down. Good readers are able to flexibly apply a wide range of comprehension strategies. Findings show that comprehension can be taught in all content areas. Teaching should emphasize *strategic* reading to spur thinking and solve problems. Varied instructional approaches are effective, including teacher modeling.

THE REALITY   Some of this good thinking has gotten misconstrued in classroom practice. Some programs overblow strategy instruction to the point that it perverts what readers naturally do and eats up so much instructional time that actual reading and classroom discussion of a text's meaning is crowded out in the never-ending competition for time. In her staff development DVD *It's ALL About Comprehension*, Sharon Taberski (2009) contends that a more useful way to think about comprehension instruction is that phonemic awareness, phonics, fluency, and vocabulary fall under the umbrella of comprehension.

Children do not learn phonics just to "do" phonics but to "use" phonics to interact meaningfully with real texts. The goal is not to ask students to sound out words but to use this knowledge to make sense of the reading. Ultimately, this is always the goal of reading. Instruction is more effective when teachers interweave the pillars to support the goal of making meaning rather than teach each one in isolation, but this has not been the case. If the goal of instruction is writing a missing vowel in workbooks or sounding out letters that are rarely connected to real texts, there is little chance that it will transfer to reading with meaning. Reading without understanding is a fruitless effort, but comprehension is often viewed as a separate pillar to be addressed after other skills are achieved.

Taking a Wider View

There is no question that the NRP pillars have had a significant impact on how we view instruction. Yet the panel offered surprisingly few specific teaching recommendations, leaving teachers to figure this out on their own. And although the NRP report tries to use language that suggests a broader view, such as cautioning against making phonics the dominant feature of the reading program, this has not had the intended effect. Many schools have adopted the narrow view emphasized in the most popular and often scripted and directive reading programs, and a smorgasbord of isolated skill-and-drill activities abound. I can imagine the ripple of excitement that washed over developers of phonics programs when the NRP report was published, an excitement that continues with RTI. We made a mistake with NCLB, but RTI is our opportunity to change direction. If we're smart, we'll jump on this opportunity as quickly as we can and refute any practice that reduces reading to nonsense.

We can begin by establishing clear descriptors with specific guidelines for more flexible implementation. It's worth emphasizing that creating a teacher's guide does not automatically mean it has a purposeful intent, encourages engagement, or uses appropriate texts. More important, it does not ensure that teachers are integrating reading into all content areas. There is no better time to learn about print than when recording ideas in a math journal or figuring out new words in a book about sharks. Literacy is a dynamic process that can be embedded throughout the school day using meaningful reading and writing activities.

In addition to questioning the relative values of the "big five," one must question the panel's decision not to review other "topics judged to be of central importance in teaching children to read" because there wasn't enough time. This has led to an increasing concern that the pillars represent a narrow view of literacy that leads to programs that are equally narrow.

> Imagine a beach house designed for construction with a foundation of ten pilings. What if insufficient funds or time constraints caused it to be built with only five pilings as its base? No one would be surprised if the house collapsed during the first strong storm. Yet that seems to be the case in reading instruction. (ALLINGTON 2005, 3)

In spite of the panel's admission of its restricted view of literacy elements, schools across the country are assuming that instruction can be limited to these five, often isolated, factors. Equally critical factors that the panel never addressed, other than to list twenty of them, remain largely untapped in many schools. Five additional elements suggested by Allington (2005, 2009) are particularly pertinent to RTI:

- **Classroom organization.** Instructional differentiation is not possible unless teachers employ a wide range of flexible grouping practices, including whole-group, small-group, and side-by-side teaching. The emphasis on programs has made whole-group instruction by far the most prevalent, as other forms of instruction are excluded.

- **Matching pupils to texts.** Few things are more critical to reading success than giving students books they are able to read. If the sole form of instruction is whole group using a single text, this becomes impossible. Students should read books at appropriate levels throughout most of the school day, not simply when they are lucky enough to get them at home or in extra-curricular settings.

- **Access to interesting texts, choice, and collaboration.** In addition to having desks filled with books at appropriate levels, students need to be able to choose some of the books they read. Kids need time to browse an array of texts that interest them and discuss them with peers in meaningful ways. They need time to participate as real-world readers rather than to complete a book report or worksheet. Reading is inherently a social act.

- *Writing and reading.* The reciprocal nature of reading and writing provides the perfect opportunity to integrate both into the literacy program and all content areas. When students spend much of their day reading and writing, they are learning about reading through their writing and vice versa. The benefits abound.

- *Expert tutoring.* This is particularly relevant in a multitiered model of instruction, in which students are taught in varied settings. The success of those instructional activities largely depends on the quality of the experiences. This makes it essential that struggling readers receive high-quality instruction from teachers well versed in literacy, so that the time devoted to these additional supports is time well spent.

As we work to build a solid foundation for RTI, these additional components are critical. This is not to suggest that the five pillars in the NRP report are not relevant, but that other, equally important factors are being largely ignored. Looking at RTI from many angles—classroom organization, student motivation and engagement, integrated approaches to curriculum and instruction—gives us the perfect opportunity to ensure that these additional key factors of literacy will be acknowledged and addressed within that framework.

The notion of RTI as a *framework* is important as it emphasizes a flexible approach as we build a foundation from the ground up. We can take advantage of worthy programs designed to support instruction, but RTI makes it more important than ever to provide teachers with the opportunities to gain the knowledge and experience to move beyond these resources. Research has shown time after time that it is teachers rather than programs that make the difference. Shouldn't people warrant at least as much faith as paper?

This emphasis on set programs is exacerbated by the notion that schools need a distinct RTI program for every grade level. Almost every major publisher offers grade-designated programs. Unfortunately, having a different program for each grade makes consistency and coordination between grades very difficult, if not impossible. Worse, it is almost guaranteed to confuse teachers and students, since the instructional focus changes every year. In fact, shouldn't it be the needs of students that serve as the basis for our instructional actions and decisions? Graduated instruction does not mean separate instruction. The goal is that each support builds on and enhances the next *with* appropriate texts in the mix.

GREEN

Widening the RTI Framework to Accommodate Exemplary Literacy Practices

Recent research has produced a wealth of information on effective literacy teaching. Implementing RTI requires viewing this research with wider understanding, however; we need to place RTI within a context of excellent authentic classroom teaching and learning practices. We have to ask ourselves, given what we know about effective literacy, how can the RTI framework build on and extend this knowledge while remaining flexible enough to accommodate varied viewpoints and professional decision making?

One point of agreement among researchers is the recognition that each child is different. We cannot then conclude that there is only one way to approach learning, particularly with struggling readers. Many schools expend time and energy trying to determine which package is the perfect recipe, but the beauty of a framework is that it *isn't* a recipe. A framework requires a descriptive view of the key features of literacy while maintaining wiggle room within this view. The framework provides the structure on which we hang thoughtful and proven approaches to reach every child.

RTI could be the powerful literacy framework needed to address the needs of all students in an effective, timely manner. The challenge is how to establish a flexible framework that effectively addresses the needs of all students. RTI can help each school craft a menu of research-based options while maintaining the role of teacher as decision maker, not disseminator. We need a framework that makes room for instructional practices that can be implemented within that framework. This requires high quality, flexible resources.

The intent of RTI is to ensure that students receive rich literacy experiences every year in every setting with every teacher, not merely in some years in some settings with some teachers.

The goal of any RTI framework is to broaden instructional alternatives, settings, and support systems for delivering instruction *before* special education services are considered. In fact, as Allington points out, "The goal of RTI legislation is to reduce the number of students who are referred for special education services" (2009, 22). A powerful feature of RTI is making literacy a schoolwide responsibility—every teacher is accountable for effective instruction for every child. The intent of RTI is to ensure that students receive rich literacy experiences *every* year in *every* setting with *every* teacher, not merely in some years in some settings with some teachers.

An effective RTI literacy framework meets the following criteria.

- ***It maintains a healthy balance between explicit skill instruction, guided practice, and independent application.*** The RTI framework

GREEN

supports varied instructional practices that reflect the gradual release of responsibility (Pearson and Gallagher 1983). Learning occurs through teacher modeling, shared and guided instructional support, and independent practice. Explicit instruction allows teachers to intentionally demonstrate important reading skills and strategies to build a solid foundation. Teachers can than offer a diminishing system of support with shared or guided reading as students apply and practice these skills and gradually transfer their learning to independent use. Independent application is the end goal.

- **RTI casts differentiation as integral.** RTI makes the classroom teacher the primary provider of thoughtful and well-planned intervention. This is impossible if the predominant form of instruction is whole group. RTI must include flexible grouping that allows teachers to target instructional needs and adjust instruction within and beyond the general curriculum. This includes a wide variety of homogeneous and heterogeneous small-group experiences, such as carefully organized day-to-day guided reading, student conferences, and side-by-side activities. Teachers will need professional development support to effectively orchestrate the varied experiences that avoid a one-size-fits-all mentality. Perhaps the very reason so many children struggle initially is this all-encompassing approach to instruction, where the core reading text is often too difficult.

- **It embeds learning in a wide range of authentic literacy experiences.** Instruction includes teacher-directed, teacher-supported, and independent activities, such as teacher read-aloud, shared and guided reading, independent reading, and peer collaboration. Learning experiences revolve around meaningful, high-interest resources and active student participation rather than passive learning and trivial paper-and-pencil tasks such as worksheets. Rich learning places students at the center, reading authentically and discussing real books. These experiences illustrate the view that reading is relevant and pleasurable and imparts this message to students.

- **It emphasizes quality talk through daily sustained discussions.** Teacher- and peer-supported discussion revolves around interesting resources that promote high-level thinking. Good teachers use these collaborations as rich springboards to thinking. They value teacher-supported whole-group, small-group, and peer activities that make talk central. Unfortunately, the increasing demands that come with teaching to the test have led teachers to abandon effective activities like small-group literature circles in favor of whole-group directed discussions. The stories in basal programs are emphasized, while more authentic and engaging material that promotes higher thinking is ignored. Worse, teachers are often told what questions to ask, discouraging the natural dialogue that arises during authentic discussions.

- ***RTI emphasizes the thinking process behind successful comprehension.***
  Good teachers purposefully build strategic knowledge into their literature
  and writing lessons and reinforce a range of effective meaning-making
  strategies such as using semantic, structural, and visual cues to figure out
  text challenges; reading between the lines; using phonetic clues to figure out
  tricky words; or calling on one's prior knowledge. They focus on understanding by using every opportunity to promote active reading through think-
  alouds and other demonstrations; and teacher-supported, peer-supported,
  and independent learning. They capitalize on the reading-writing connection,
  engaging students in writing short, simple texts that students can then use to
  practice reading. They purposefully reinforce knowledge or reteach to bring
  about understanding.

- ***It is rooted in an environment that reinforces and extends learning.***
  Students actively participate in a range of meaningful experiences, independently or with peers, that reinforce and extend learning. Management systems exist not to control students, but rather to promote independent
  engagement in meaningful literacy that continues even when teachers leave
  the room or meet with a small group of students. Fluency work promotes
  meaning and builds deeper levels of understanding rather than focusing on
  speed. Activities that emphasize meaning and celebrate repeated reading,
  such as readers theater, dramatic reading, and peer sharing, are valued, and
  blocks of time are dedicated each day for these critical experiences.

- ***It gives students a prominent role in their own learning.*** Effective
  teachers know that learning cannot be about mastery if it remains a mystery.
  They have high expectations and make these expectations clear as students
  become co-collaborators. They engage students in generating essential learning goals and rubrics, charts, and other ongoing references to guide reflective conversations. They view student conferences as opportunities to reflect
  on past and current goals or establish new directions. Effective teachers encourage students to use peer- and self-assessment to celebrate successes and
  set new goals. They illuminate learning through explanations and carefully
  planned activities rather than label it with happy faces and red marks. They
  spend time demonstrating skills and providing support as children acquire
  new learning through ongoing feedback and guidance.

- ***It supports the reality that motivation and learning are inseparable.***
  Effective teachers refuse to buy into the misconception that independent
  reading of self-selected texts is a poor use of time. They enrich these experiences with guidance and feedback and recognize the value of reading easy,
  interesting texts over dull grade-level ones. They believe a classroom library is
  essential to a well-balanced learning environment, and teach students how

to access it on their own. They celebrate reading workshop as a way to encourage independent reading, confer with students, and offer immediate feedback. They recognize that the potential for learning increases the more students are motivated to learn, and they create an environment to nurture this motivation.

- *It emphasizes resources at appropriate levels of challenge.* Students are not subjected to texts and tasks that are frustrating; instructional support and scaffolds are in place to ensure that every experience is pleasurable and meaningful. Massive numbers of interesting narrative and expository texts are available. Instructional activities revolve around slightly challenging enrichment texts and teacher-supported learning, reinforced by texts students can read independently. Teachers don't give grade-level texts to students who are reading below grade level; they use supplementary resources that acknowledge context, instructional setting, and level of support as essential considerations. In short, teachers ensure that every student has books that they can—and want to—read. Successful reading experiences are paramount.

Coming Full Circle

It's hardly a surprise that teachers today feel torn between sound beliefs and political realities. We have a rich understanding of what constitutes effective literacy and can enhance that understanding through great quantities of information in books and on the Web. We have unending resources at our disposal and sellers of instructional programs vying for our attention. But we're also frustrated. We must often do the right thing behind closed doors and play the political game as soon as the door opens. We balance professional responsibility with an onrush of demands competing for time. We sense the loss of control but are reluctant to talk about it for fear of recrimination.

YELLOW

Many view RTI as one more frustration—but this is a hasty conclusion. *If we proceed with caution*, RTI has the *potential* to return decision making where it belongs—with teachers. RTI has the *potential* to make literacy a shared responsibility through respectful collaboration and dialogue. Again, picture a crossroad. One road takes us toward blind compliance and allegiance to mandated programs implemented rigidly. The other road is a longer route that has rest stops and side roads and is one on which programs and professional judgment can respectfully coexist. Which road do we take? Schools *do* have a choice; that choice determines whether history repeats itself or we create a new reality where the best of everything is welcome.

Let me return to where I began this chapter. I see the looks of fear on the faces of my audience as I prepare to talk about RTI. As I begin to speak, teachers begin to take notes. Of all the points they may have jotted down, here are the positive take-aways I want them—and you—to remember most as you read on. RTI promises to:

- Give struggling learners the same opportunities as the strongest readers to engage in meaningful literacy.

- Incorporate programs that are of the highest quality and flexible enough to include teacher judgement.

- Provide teachers with a wide repertoire of rich strategies that make room for instructional choices and options according to the needs of each child.

- Create an instructional framework that will guide teachers' efforts to address all students' needs using flexible supports.

- Generate ongoing support systems to assist teachers as they learn to implement RTI more effectively.

- Accommodate consistency and coordination by making sure that each tier of RTI builds on and enhances the next.

- Increase collaboration and professional dialogue between and among classroom teachers and interventionists at all grade levels.

The summer before my first "teachers" arrived, I planted a tiny garden outside my classroom. In the subsequent afternoons, as cows roamed nearby, I watched my garden grow. I came to see that the garden inside my classroom depended on my choices as much as the one outside did. My students mirrored my flowers, growing unpredictably but flourishing in their own way in the end. I think often about the seeds I planted in small-town Missouri. I am grateful to the twelve students who instilled in me an intense desire to learn about literacy, a thirst I'll never stop trying to quench.

RTI: A Framework for Responsive Differentiated Teaching

*S*uccessful gardening is doing what has to be done when it has to be done the way it ought to be done whether you want to do it or not.

—*Jerry Baker*

You're walking down the hallway of a school that has successfully put a response to intervention framework in place. There is something in the air—a positive energy. A hum of activity ripples through the building. You peer into a classroom and see first graders gathered around their teacher as they read aloud the poem displayed on an easel, their voices rising and falling with the cadences of the verse. Students take turns pointing to words as everyone reads along. Then the teacher writes several words from the poem on a chart, and they exchange observations about the poet's words, rhymes, and spelling patterns, noting the wonderful "bounce" of words when they're read aloud. After a few minutes they turn back to the poem to do one more choral reading of the now familiar rhyme.

Next, the class disperses to other areas of the room. They collect materials and begin working alone or with a partner. Three students gather around a table with the teacher. After rereading the same poem, they make words with magnetic letters. The three students then carefully record each word on a small whiteboard, slowly repeating the word before writing it. The teacher responds to their efforts. They read the poem once again before returning to their seats. Four new students take their places. I watch as children continue to meet in small groups or one-on-one for needed support. The teacher, like a conductor, orchestrates purposeful instruction that is meaningful and relevant for each child.

This description provides a glimpse of how an RTI framework allows educators to make the most of every minute and design a range of approaches to meet the needs of students. The RTI we need does not require everyone to read the same book, complete the same task, and be on the same page in scripted, whole-class sameness. In fact, *that* RTI would be little better than the status quo. The RTI that will bring struggling readers up to the level of their peers is a powerful organizational structure for learning that accommodates all children, gifted and struggling alike. Each child is an active participant in authentic literacy experiences that take their interests and differences into account. The RTI we need broadens instructional options to place the focus on maximizing achievement for *all* students.

How do we build this organizational structure? By putting good instruction at the forefront of our minds, and realizing how much we can do in tier 1. Chapter 3 will delve into the instructional piece in more detail, but for now, consider that response to *instruction* may be a more appropriate name for RTI (Allington 2008). Effective reading instruction incorporates intervention, but RTI should be about what takes place all day long for every student, rather than during a narrow time frame for a select group of students.

The term *compliance* is frequently used in discussions of RTI. Don't forget that this term also implies excessive acquiescence or submission without protest. Try not to let this word infiltrate the conceptualizing of a thoughtful RTI plan in your school that includes teachers as decision makers.

RED

Saying Good-Bye to the "Wait to Fail" Model

I began my career as a special education teacher and still have vivid memories of the many challenges of accessing support for struggling readers. Many classroom teachers were ill prepared to meet the needs of unique learners, and quickly referred students to special education. Because the referral process was extremely rigid and lengthy, and special education teachers typically had large caseloads; students were either forced to play a waiting game in the regular classroom or received the services of an aide.

When these students finally were tested, many of their diagnostic assessments found no discrepancy between IQ and performance; those students were returned to the classroom and a teacher who received limited support and few resources with which to address students' needs. Some of these students were later referred successfully for additional support, but by this time the achievement gap had widened significantly and was exacerbated by a growing sense of failure propelled by the ongoing struggle.

When students did qualify for special education, they usually received support that supplanted rather than extended or complemented the classroom program—this resulted in *separate*, not *additional*, instruction, and there was little consistency between this disconnected effort and the regular classroom. The adults, all committed to supporting a child, rarely collaborated.

But let's assume the student receiving special education responded to the support and the performance gap began to close. A new diagnostic test showed that a discrepancy no longer existed. The reward for this gain was to remove the support and the child returned to the classroom! Rather than giving teachers the opportunity to work together, the child was left to make sense of the two opposing worlds.

This "wait to fail" model generally led to support that was too little, too late, and too limited. Special education was a place children were sent to be "fixed" by programs that were largely ineffective and had little connection to the regular classroom; students then spent the remainder of the day in the regular classroom, where the teacher knew little about the instruction they received in special education. Little time or attention was given to encouraging special education and regular classroom teachers to work together. The result was fragmentation, incoherence, and children caught in the middle.

RTI can address the problems associated with this model. It returns responsibility for students who are struggling to classroom teachers who receive the professional support and resources necessary to address their students' learning needs. It ensures that special education does not become a place where children go to be "fixed." Rather, it encourages teachers to work together to ensure that any special education referrals are legitimate. In short, RTI is designed to create schools that support *all* students.

An Overview of RTI Tiers

The RTI Action Network (www.rtinetwork.org) describes RTI as "a multitiered approach to help struggling learners. Student progress is closely monitored at

An Overview of the Three-Tiered Model of RTI

The three-tiered model is the most common RTI design. A tiered model is an effective design to offer instructional support at increasing levels of intensity according to student need, and with specific features:

TIER 1: UNIVERSAL OR GENERAL EDUCATION
- about 80 percent
- all students
- flexible grouping and differentiated instruction

TIER 2: TARGETED OR SUPPLEMENTAL
- 10 to 15 percent
- small group not to exceed five
- one thirty-minute daily session

TIER 3: STRATEGIC OR INTENSIVE
- 5 to 10 percent
- individualized or very small group not to exceed three
- two thirty-minute daily sessions

each stage of intervention to determine the need for further research-based instruction and/or intervention in general education, in special education, or both." The number of tiers varies from school to school, but three tiers are most common. In a sense, tiers also offer a safety net for struggling teachers, since ongoing assessment and referral to higher tiers quickly reveal where large percentages of students are not making progress.

TIER 1 Tier 1 intervention takes place in the regular classroom and offers the earliest support. It is the "universal" tier, or the general education program. By assessing the total student population three times annually, schools are more likely to identify and monitor students at risk of failure. Tier 1 emphasizes a high-quality general curriculum as well as differentiated instruction; flexible grouping is key. Specific instructional interventions are implemented for students who are not likely to achieve success with grade-level curriculum and texts, and ongoing assessment is used to determine the level of success of interventions and suggest necessary changes.

In an RTI framework, the regular classroom teacher is integral to the instructional progress of all students, regardless of other supports in place. Because not all teachers have the expertise to meet varying instructional needs, teacher support—both in-class assistance and professional development—is critical to children's success. By focusing on teacher support, tier 1 offers the opportunity to meet the needs of all students rather than referring them to higher intervention tiers.

TIER 2 Students who do not respond to general interventions, even with appropriate adjustments, may be moved to tier 2 for an additional thirty minutes of instruction daily in small groups (up to five students, although three or fewer is preferred). This instruction is provided by the classroom teacher or someone else, during or after school, within or outside the classroom. These determinations are based on a school's available resources.

Tier 2 instruction offers more targeted support that generally revolves around a specific area of need (vocabulary, for example), as much as possible emphasizing skills and strategies in meaningful contexts. Again, progress is monitored through ongoing data collection and informal assessment. Tier 2 instruction is temporary, although it may be offered in several rounds. However, a student's progress in tier 2 is largely dependent on the collaboration of those providing support.

TIER 3 Tier 3 is the highest level of support and is targeted to meet the specific needs of the small percentage of students who are still unsuccessful. Two additional thirty-minute instructional sessions are offered daily. Support is more individualized by reducing the instructional setting to three or fewer and often one-on-one. Tier 3 instruction should be provided by a highly qualified reading teacher, generally outside the classroom. Progress is monitored more frequently, but care must be taken that testing does not take the place of teaching.

RTI experts disagree whether tier 3 is special education or a precursor to it. I will illustrate in Chapter 5 why tier 3 should be considered a more intensive level of support *prior* to special education to provide an additional support option. If the top tier in an RTI model is special education, another tier should be added, so that special education becomes tier 4. This makes special education an option that is related to but outside of the basic tiered framework. Teachers who support children in all tiers must make a commitment to work collaboratively to ensure students do not receive confusing or even conflicting instruction.

Detailed descriptions of each tier are provided in Chapter 3 (tier 1), Chapter 4 (tier 2), and Chapter 5 (tier 3). I struggled with whether to discuss the tiers in separate chapters, since they are inseparable in practice. Nevertheless, separating them makes it easier to illustrate key points and clarify distinctions. Let me stress, however, that movement between tiers is not linear—the tiers are interrelated, and when particular students enter and exit a tier varies. Details such as how long a child stays at a tier, who provides support at each tier, or what the next step is must remain flexible. The important thing is that instruction in all tiers is interconnected to promote strategies and skills across the curriculum and reinforce this learning in multiple contexts. This interdependence breaks down previous support barriers and encourages more seamless integration of instruction within and between tiers. Just remember the acronym LEARN:

LINK: Ensure that the support provided at each tier is interrelated with other tiers. For example, Robert is introduced to a new instructional strategy at tier 3. The classroom teacher highlights this same strategy during differentiated instruction.

ENGAGE: Emphasize activities that make students active participants in learning. For example, Julian learns vocabulary in the context of real books rather than passive worksheets. She is immersed in this learning through authentic reading and writing experiences in a wide variety of settings.

ACCELERATE: Intensify learning experiences at all tiers for accelerated progress. For example, Dominique's teacher knows every minute counts. Each learning activity is designed to extend existing knowledge or promote new learning with teacher-supported, scaffolded experiences such as guided reading.

REINFORCE: Emphasize reinforcement and practice within and across every tier. For example, Todd learns how to use picture clues to figure out unknown words at tier 2. The classroom teacher ensures that he has ample guided practice and then reinforces this learning in other contexts to promote transfer of knowledge.

NEGOTIATE: Adjust the tiers to fit your school and staff given existing resources. For example, Lincoln School pays teachers a stipend to conduct tiered support before school. The school also purchased a wide range of quality science and social studies texts to integrate reading into content-area subjects and thus maximize the day.

Pull-Out Versus Push-In

Tier 1 interventions generally occur in the classroom, with or without the support of other staff members. The appropriate time and location for tier 2 and 3 interventions, which supplement the general education reading program,

YELLOW

require careful thought as these decisions depend on the needs of students. Blanket decisions will not be effective because they do not take these needs into account. One important caution: minimize the number of adults working with an individual child. Too often children become confused because they receive conflicting instruction.

The three usual location options are in-class, pull-out, or push-in. In-class interventions, typical of tier 1, are the responsibility of the classroom teacher, while tier 2 interventions may be offered with or without professional support. Pull-out interventions, typical of tiers 2 and 3, take place outside the classroom. Push-in interventions are conducted by support staff in the regular classroom, typically at tiers 1 and 2. I would argue that a fourth and often preferable option is a combination of the three in that the setting should be adjusted according to instructional goals and student needs. For example, a pull-out approach may be used to set the stage for learning or reinforce new learning, while a push-in approach will help children transfer this learning to the general curriculum.

We need to begin by considering the advantages and disadvantages of a push-in or pull-out approach. (The chart in Figure 2.1 gives a brief overview.) Since RTI is a relatively new approach, there is little research to support one option over the other. Title 1 pull-out programs have resulted in small annual gains, but this may stem from the way these programs are typically designed: they are separate from the classroom program, focus on skill and drill, and often lead to long-term support. Tier 2 and 3 interventions in the RTI model are short-term, emphasize high-quality instruction with appropriate texts, are coordinated between tiers, and focus on acceleration so students can return to the regular classroom program as soon as possible. Reading Recovery is an example of an effective pull-out model, particularly given the ongoing professional support designed to increase these benefits.

Many of the disadvantages associated with each option can be easily addressed. If noise is an issue with a push-in program, for example, the classroom teacher can institute more effective classroom procedures. Collaboration is certainly more difficult with a pull-out model, but a push-in program will not necessarily be coordinated any better. On the other hand, some disadvantages are more difficult to address, such as travel time lost with a pull-out program. Lost time is inevitable and can be extensive when students must travel to and from the classroom. These are all important considerations; there is no single perfect answer.

One of the biggest dangers of a tier 2 or 3 push-in approach is the temptation to supplant tier 1 interventions by the classroom teacher, especially if the higher-tier interventions are scheduled during literacy instruction. It is also

Figure 2.1 Advantages and Disadvantages of Push-In and Pull-Out Interventions

PUSH-IN ADVANTAGES	PULL-OUT ADVANTAGES
• Increases instructional continuity • Is unobtrusive • Doesn't require moving to another location • Ensures time is spent on instruction rather than travel • Provides a model for instruction • Encourages shared planning • Can be coordinated with the general curriculum	• Involves fewer distractions • Provides another perspective • Easier to schedule beyond classroom reading instruction • Provides the special attention of a support teacher • May increase student engagement • Makes it easier to emphasize supplemental material
PUSH-IN DISADVANTAGES	**PULL-OUT DISADVANTAGES**
• Requires buy-in by everyone involved • Takes place in a crowded classroom • Is susceptible to distractions • May supplant tier 1 instruction • Could view expert teachers as glorified aides • Emphasizes grade-level material	• Requires additional space • Requires travel time (lost instruction time) • Creates scheduling difficulties • Makes collaboration more challenging • Creates the stigma of leaving the classroom • Does not encourage shared ideas

more likely that grade-level material will be used in a push-in approach—care should be taken to match texts to students. Children should not be pulled out of reading instruction or from desirable activities like recess. Regardless of the option selected, teacher buy-in is essential. The key is to ensure time for collaboration and planning by those involved in each support tier (Ferguson 1992).

In short, either option may be effective if the staff takes the time and energy to consider and address all the factors involved, while both options will be ineffective without collaboration and the use of appropriate texts and well-designed instructional strategies. Emphasis must be on high-quality experiences to accelerate learning and get students back into classrooms quickly. This means that every instructional activity should be carefully chosen with a focus on immersing students in meaningful learning experiences with carefully selected texts. The decision must always be based on what is best for that particular student, not on what is convenient for the school or teachers.

The Changing Face of RTI

The roots of RTI can be traced back thirty years, with a more recent boost from the reauthorization of the Individuals with Disabilities Education Act of 2004 (IDEA). The purpose of this book is not to explore RTI's history; this has been done very thoroughly by other authors (Bender and Shores 2007; Brown-Chidsey and Steege 2005). Simply put, RTI emphasizes high-quality instruction in conjunction with ongoing data to determine whether students *respond* to instruction.

Let's look at some basic premises of RTI:

- RTI makes literacy a schoolwide responsibility with a focus on early identification; schools can then intervene at the first sign of problems rather than wait until the learning gap widens.

- RTI does not label students or relegate them to a program; rather, it makes *all* teachers accountable for high-quality instruction *and* differentiation.

- RTI supports cautious selection of interventions using data to inform instruction; this creates a safety net for struggling readers.

- RTI uses ongoing assessment to gauge how students respond to interventions in and across tiers; instruction is then adjusted accordingly.

- RTI is based on the premise that *all* children can learn if appropriate support is available; there are no acceptable losses.

- RTI creates a framework that makes each teacher responsible for students *before* support alternatives are even considered.

In essence, RTI reflects what good teachers have always done as they design effective instruction: they identify a problem, devise a plan to address the problem, analyze the success of the plan, and establish new goals (see Figure 2.2).

The success of RTI hinges on the expectation that every teacher can become an effective literacy teacher. Of course, we must back up this expectation by offering ongoing professional development, thoughtful materials, and teacher support, or there is little chance of its success.

We can identify nine key features of response to intervention.

Key Features of RTI

1. RTI aligns the support options within and outside the regular classroom. This design offers students the most appropriate schoolwide instruction.

2. RTI screens the entire student population three times during the year. Students who may not be successful with the grade-level curriculum are identified, intervention is planned and offered, and progress is monitored over time.

Figure 2.2 The Cycle
of Effective Teaching

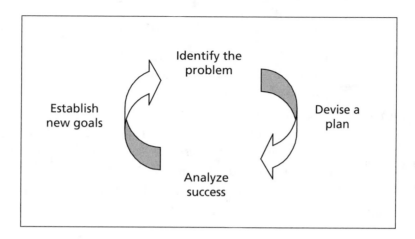

3. RTI emphasizes early intervention and ongoing assessment. Students at risk are identified at the earliest stages so that specific instruction can be planned.

4. RTI provides interventions at increasing levels of intensity. A variety of support options are provided before special education is considered.

5. RTI continuously monitors and documents progress, using a variety of assessments that determine how much and under what conditions children learn.

6. RTI incorporates general education and supplemental high-quality instruction matched to students' needs.

7. RTI ensures success for all students through carefully selected, appropriate instructional support options.

8. RTI is a collaborative effort using a problem-solving team approach. The team makes specific decisions about what, when, where, and how instruction is provided.

9. RTI provides ongoing professional development. Reading specialists or coaches model instructional methods and provide in-class support. Teachers need demonstrations in the same way students do.

Essential Principles of RTI

An RTI framework used flexibly makes room for varied interpretations that take into account unique school populations, the knowledge and preparation of staff members, and available resources. While this flexibility alarms those who insist on precision, it is a rich feature of RTI that should be maintained. The essential principles outlined below should guide schools or districts as they create their framework (these points are elaborated on in later chapters).

Time Is a Precious Commodity

The decision to use any learning activity must be based on a conscious evaluation that it is worth the time required.

Every minute spent on RTI should count. We all have the same limited amount of time, yet some choose to waste it. Some principals demand that students take computerized tests on each book they read and tout this testing as good instruction. Some teachers distribute stacks of worksheets and cut-and-paste activities as a substitute for authentic learning. The decision to use any learning activity must be based on a conscious evaluation that it is worth the time required. RTI brings with it a heightened awareness of the ticking clock; all decisions must respect the limited time in a school day and be focused on the critical goal of decreasing the achievement gap. Our choices matter!

This means we must begin by identifying the values that will drive the school day. What are your "nonnegotiables," the things you hold highest in importance? Write them down (if your emphasis is on isolated skill-and-drill activities, it's time to reevaluate your thinking!). Do packaged programs reflect your values, or is your day spent engaging students in learning activities that really matter, such as time for students to read real books at appropriate levels? Make authentic activities a high priority by building your schedule around them and ensure you have the resources to support these events.

One Size Fits Few

This term, borrowed from Susan Ohanian (1999), celebrates the idea that each child brings something unique to the literacy table. If we can agree on this point, we must also agree that each child's needs can't be met in the same way. Quality resources that suggest activities and materials are very effective in the hands of knowledgeable professionals who use them flexibly or can serve as a safety net for less experienced teachers as they develop a deeper understanding of literacy. However, common sense also dictates that these resources are inadequate for meeting unique needs, as there are invariably students who are reading well below or above grade level. Differentiation, dynamic and varied grouping, and alternative resources are critical to the success of RTI—and ultimately to the success of students.

I'm not sure why providing books students *can* read is a point of contention, but it has become a heated argument in education. Daily doses of successful experiences with texts is the single most important thing we can do to make RTI work. If ever the courage was needed to "go against the grain," (Allington 2002) by moving away from scripted guides and whole-group, grade-level texts, now is the time. Students need texts and tasks at appropriate levels every day, all day. We can and must modify learning to guarantee success every day or *leaving no child behind* is a meaningless expression.

Intensity Is the Great Equalizer

In a multitiered RTI model, the bulk of instruction is provided in the regular classroom, focuses on effective literacy practices, and meets the needs of all students. Every child is assessed, initially and over time, through informal observation and during conferences, and those who are likely to need additional support are identified. The goal of schoolwide assessment is not to label or segregate students, but to support instructional design and planning that allow us to accommodate individual needs.

Obviously, classroom instruction is insufficient for some students. Additional, more intense instructional support is then offered. Tier 2 and 3 support decreases group size and devotes more time to more targeted learning experiences. Schools determine who offers this higher-tier support, but the professionals who do should have appropriate qualifications. Collaboration between classroom teachers and interventionists increases RTI effectiveness, so time should be built into the day for this purpose. Adequate time and appropriate resources will make or break the high-quality instructional support our students deserve.

The Power of "Double Dipping"

The degree to which a tiered model succeeds depends on the relationship between tiers. If tiers 2 and 3 *replace* tier 1, instruction will be *instead of* rather than *in addition to* the classroom curriculum. This simply moves learning from one setting to another, which is not the intent of RTI. Rather, higher tiers of support are a shared responsibility of classroom teachers and build on what has been accomplished in the classroom. The goal is to offer *more*—more time, more support, and more opportunity. Students at higher tiers continue to receive tier 1 support. This is the basis of *double dipping*, or providing both classroom and alternative support concurrently.

This interrelatedness requires coordination between supports so that the efforts at different tiers are not at cross-purposes but reinforce learning at deeper levels of understanding in multiple contexts. Open professional communication between tiers is essential as ongoing dialogue reframes *yours versus mine* as *ours*: what can *we* do to ensure the success of *our* students? This shared responsibility means students can seamlessly integrate their learning from tier 2 or 3 instruction into any activity at tier 1.

Transfer Is the Glue

Obviously, the end goal of instruction is for students to "own" new knowledge. Teaching on the surface is tempting, particularly with curriculum bulging at the seams. To avoid this, we must promote strategies and skills (Afflerbach et al. 2008). Strategies are conscious plans a reader initiates, with or without support, to solve problems that occur within the context of reading. They are deliberate and goal directed. Skills are strategies that have become automatic actions a reader takes unconsciously, or without awareness. Skills develop with repeated practice. Students *transfer* learning when they apply it to another text, task, or context.

Most basal programs practice a "more is more" mentality when *more is really less.* Many teachers feel bombarded with increasing demands. One school I visited requires two separate reading programs in addition to the general curriculum, leaving little room for professional judgment. We must leave time for critical features of RTI, such as coordination between support tiers. This integration promotes practice and emphasizes a gradual release of responsibility (Pearson and Gallagher 1983) through teacher modeling (*I do*), shared and guided practice (*we do*), and independent application (*you do*). Unless this essential transfer is the end goal of teaching, our efforts will be wasted.

Data Collection: Finding a Middle Ground

Assessment poses the greatest challenge in implementing RTI. It is addressed in detail in Chapter 6, but a brief discussion here sets the stage for the description of tiers in the next three chapters.

Universal assessment, or screening—conducted three times a year—is a key feature of RTI. Student progress is monitored throughout instruction to determine effectiveness. Ongoing assessment increases accountability and ensures our students make adequate progress. Without question, these are both worthy goals.

Alas, the assessment piece of RTI has the potential to get co-opted by commerce—lucrative assessment products are a real danger. They are not necessarily sound, not necessarily necessary—and they have the potential to take valuable instructional time. A recommendation of daily progress monitoring runs the risk that assessment will take over the instructional process. Even with one-minute probes, time adds up quickly. This is not to say that assessments are not important. But we must always examine whether they actually increase the quality of instruction. This is not always the case.

Assessments can provide useful information for important instructional decisions. Unfortunately, this is rarely the case if schools focus exclusively on numerical values. The problem is that identical scores can paint the same picture when the reality is different. Valencia and Buly illustrated this point by exploring the varied instructional needs of students who achieved the same test scores. They stated, "Simply knowing which children have failed state tests is a bit like knowing that you have a fever when you are feeling ill, but having no idea of the cause or cure" (2005, 134).

Data collection emphasized in RTI can also draw attention away from more authentic forms of assessment. The frustration of attempting to monitor children's progress can lead teachers to abandon deeper levels of assessment. This is unfortunate, considering that the more assessment moves away from real reading, the less information we glean from it. Assessment designed to inform instruction is connected to the reading process, not separate from it or isolated to a single measure. Effective assessment occurs in daily instructional contexts and supports future instructional decisions. In this way, every instructional experience offers an opportunity to learn more about students and inform practice. Summative assessments judge learners' progress. Formative assessments are continuous, ongoing, and more process oriented. Can we afford to allow RTI to crowd out these critical assessment forms?

Assessment strategies such as kid watching (Goodman et al. 1978), checklists, rubrics, anecdotal records, listening to children read, running records, student conferences, retelling, portfolios, questionnaires, surveys, literature response, and demonstrations of authentic learning in action are needed to inform, support, and drive the instructional process. We should be far more concerned about these rich sources of information than we are about data collection "tools" that focus on surface features of reading. Our best source of information is a thoughtful and skilled teacher who observes and learns from the student. I'm not suggesting we shouldn't use monitoring tools that focus on the surface features of language, but we must beware of *overusing* them to the point that more effective daily contextual assessments are swept aside. I see this happen in school after school, from state to state.

Abraham Lincoln stated, "We can complain because rose bushes have thorns, or rejoice because thorn bushes have roses." Perhaps the first goal is to identify the thorns in order to enjoy the roses more intensely. RTI comes to us with some sticky issues, but we can get around them. I like to tell teachers "the response in *response to intervention* is both our students' and our own." It's up to us to respond wisely with the very best resources, instructional strategies, and professional development to close the achievement gap. You matter!

*O*ur best source of information is a thoughtful and skilled teacher who observes and learns from the student.

Tier 1 Intervention: High-Quality Instruction for All

*N*o two gardens are the same. No two days are the same in one garden.

—*Hugh Johnson*

Juggling Elephants (Loflin and Musig 2007) is the story of a man's attempt to juggle life's responsibilities. Using a three-ring circus as a metaphor, he discovers "doing it all" is like juggling elephants—impossible. A ringmaster has the greatest impact on the success of the circus but can pay attention to only one ring at a time. Each ring contains a high-quality act. The rings are connected; what happens in one enhances the others.

The three-ring circus is a good metaphor for the challenge of tier 1 instruction. Trying to "do it all" simultaneously is like juggling elephants—impossible. Instead, as ringmaster, the teacher must ensure that each aspect of the literacy program (see Figure 3.1) represents a high-quality, interrelated function. The teacher is ever aware of all three rings, but she is able to expertly focus on

Figure 3.1 Facets of High-Quality Tier 1 Instruction

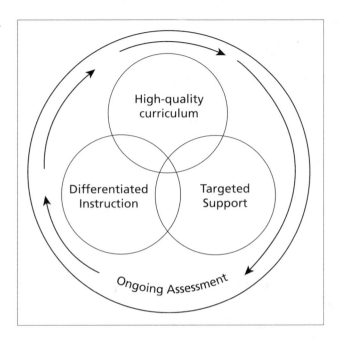

what's now in her spotlight. For example, while she attends to a reading conference, she knows that her other young readers are reading just-right books independently, or are engaged in a discussion about a picture book with which she's modeled comprehension strategies.

Essential Components of Effective Instruction

Tier 1 is often described as the universal tier since it occurs in a general education setting; it is quite simply the foundation of the school's literacy program. A common consensus is that 80 percent of students will be successful if tier 1 instruction is broad enough to meet learners' needs within *and* beyond the grade-level curriculum.

Tier 1 literacy instruction occurs in a dedicated block of time (generally between one and a half and two hours). The more expertly we attend to tier 1, the more daily action there will be in *each* instructional ring. If each ring is filled with exemplary literacy practices, less outside support will be needed. This underscores the central role of classroom teachers. On page 36 is a typical tier 1 schedule for K–3 using a reading and writing workshop model. Notice how literacy emanates from authentic reading and writing, which begins the day. This allows us to reach a wide range of readers.

Typical Daily Schedule

8:20–8:40 First Independent Reading

Children read books from informational text baskets and other book baskets around the room. The teacher does small-group reading or word work with the most "at-risk" students.

8:40–9:30 Meeting (Whole-Group Session)

Children share informational text learning from first independent reading time and do "words, words, words" vocabulary (when appropriate).

Interactive read aloud or shared reading or shared writing with a strategy or skill focus.

If you haven't tried the workshop model, it's wiser to select one of the instructional components and do it well, then add another, rather than trying to launch all the components at once.

9:30–10:30 Reading Workshop

Mini-lesson (often a recap of the skill or strategy demonstrated during read aloud, shared reading, and so on)

Reading conferences or small-group reading The teacher meets one-on-one with three to five children to advise them on what they're doing well and what they could do better and to help match them with books.

The teacher meets with a small group of readers to guide them through a text that may be too difficult for them to read on their own. She might also with a small group for interactive read aloud, literature circles, or word study groups.

Second independent reading The children read books from their book bag, work on their reading log, response sheets, or response notebook. They might also do reading-related center activities.

10:20–10:30 Reading share

Often launched with a prompt like, "What did you learn about yourself as a reader? What worked so well today that you might try to do it again and again?"

10:30–10:40 Writing Mini-Lesson or Children Sharing Pieces of Writing

10:40–11:20 Writing Workshop (includes spelling and handwriting)

Writing conferences or small-group writing

Independent writing

Writing share (11:10–11:20)

Explore such questions as, "What did you learn about yourself as a writer? What worked so well today that you might try to do it again and again?"

Adapted from Taberski, 2000, *On Solid Ground*

The ultimate aim of RTI is to reduce the number of students who are referred for special education services. To accomplish this goal, the general education program must be high quality and strive to meet students' needs through four *daily* goals:

1. Implement a high-quality, research-based general education curriculum based on expert teaching.

2. Integrate differentiated instruction using resources that extend beyond a common reading program.

3. Offer targeted, more intense instructional support by aligning assessment and classroom instruction.

4. Monitor each student's progress with continuous, reliable, and authentic formal and informal assessments that support instruction.

We move seamlessly between these goals according to students' needs at any given time.

A High-Quality Curriculum Based on Expert Teaching

I say *curriculum* rather than *core program*, because the latter seems to perpetuate the notion that we need a package. Commercial programs may have a place as resources, but they can control rather than support the spirit of good teaching. We need to think about programs more cautiously, because RTI brings on a deluge of products that can sink the initiative and once again replace thoughtful teaching. There are excellent, research-based commercial resources, but as a profession, we must resist the compulsion to follow them with little or no variance for meeting student needs. This scenario is all too common, especially in an era of Reading First and NCLB, which has failed to produce the expected gains. We must augment and improvise within and beyond programs. Just as a ringmaster is key to a successful circus, the teacher is key to a successful instructional program.

That said, *flexible* use of high-quality published programs can support expert teaching. Packaged programs offer some benefits, including grade-level resources, scope-and-sequence charts, pacing guides, and supplementary resources. If these aids are treated as instructional road maps rather than one-way streets, no detours allowed, they are rich resources that give novice teachers a supportive scaffold and allow experienced teachers to make thoughtful adjustments. A grand collaboration occurs as teachers make instructional choices to meet the needs of their students. We move from *compliant* to *responsive* if we follow sound published advice *and* teach intentionally based on what our students show us they need.

YELLOW

Beware of bad advice in teacher's guides that are sometimes written by the program's lead authors. They are sometimes written by publishing personnel, with no teaching experience. Thus, these guides can be superficial and even riddled with questionable advice. For example, a third-grade nonfiction text about snakes suggests generating *sn* words when *snake* is the only *sn* word that appears in the story. An information text on caterpillars suggests creating caterpillars from men's ties. Neither activity deepens students' content knowledge. "Before" and "after" reading activities can take more time than the actual reading and leave little time to reread or discuss. As we faithfully follow absurd suggestions that steal time from reading, we find ourselves hopelessly juggling elephants —an impossible and irresponsible task.

GETTING THE BEST FROM PUBLISHED PROGRAMS: BE A WISE CONSUMER

When using any published resource, keep your expertise in the picture. All you need is a pad of sticky notes and an open mind to customize it and take the best from its texts and teaching materials. For example, before opening the teacher's guide, read the student text and jot down ideas that come to mind. Note challenging words, logical stopping points to make predictions, questions to initiate peer discussion, and key learning concepts. Then transfer your sticky notes to the teacher's guide, replacing low-level questions and adding reflections and teachable moments the publisher missed.

This practice is effective on three counts. First, it demonstrates the value of knowing texts well before teaching. Second, it allows students' needs to guide our instructional choices as we add, modify, or even delete irrelevant suggestions. Third, it puts us in the driver's seat; we assume a lead role in instructional design with the *support* of the publisher. Just as we fail to build independent strategies if we *tell students what to do*, we fail to promote independent decision making if we rely on publishers to *tell us what to do*.

THE TROUBLE WITH A COMMON ANTHOLOGY

Having a common high-quality curriculum, differentiated to meet a class' diverse needs, is not the issue. The dilemma is using the same anthology for every child. Students read the same text, often round robin, even though the piece is out of reach for some. Regardless of the support offered, struggling readers improve their comprehension only by reading texts that match their reading level (O'Connor et al. 2002). I am unaware of any research that supports asking students to read texts with no meaning for them. To add insult to injury, stories in grade-level anthologies are often long, tedious, and accompanied by equally frustrating drills far removed from the reading.

Whole-group instruction is not inherently bad. It just can't be all that we do. The key to successful whole-group instruction is designing it so that every child can walk away a winner. It is *our* responsibility to design successful reading experiences that guarantee all students membership in the literacy club (Smith 1987). Common whole-group goals supported by flexible scaffolds are effective if student needs are taken into account and if this is *one component* of the instructional design rather than the norm. Tomlinson (1999) suggests we may begin to differentiate by not differentiating, but this is virtually impossible if we merely hand out thirty copies of grade-level material.

CREATING A BROADER INSTRUCTIONAL LANDSCAPE

Reading excellent texts aloud is one of the most effective whole-group approaches for achieving any instructional goal cited in a teacher's guide. It allows us introduce new learning to a wider range of students. Interactive read-alouds, "holding thinking" with sticky notes, and "turn and talk" practices embedded in the experience ensure student engagement and make children active participants. Generally, a read-aloud session lasts about fifteen minutes and takes the form of a mini-lesson with teacher modeling. We can then follow this with differentiated small-group or independent instruction, partner reading, or conferring to identify students in need of extra support.

Schools should also be free to use an instructional design that does *not* revolve around a program. Teachers are achieving great success with literature-based approaches such as reading workshop, in which skills or strategies are intentionally taught within meaningful, motivating instruction based on teacher-selected books (Atwell 2007; Miller 2008). The success of these experiences, carefully designed in connection with standard curriculum goals, is reflected in schoolwide test scores, yet many schools are told they cannot use these practices. I'm not sure RTI is a step forward if we abandon practices with proven track records just because they are not sold in a slick package.

Grade-level curriculum goals do not alleviate our responsibility to accommodate varied learning needs. As literacy teachers, we are fortunate that we can teach required skills in appropriate level texts. We can address coherent goals for each grade and still adjust the pathway for achieving those goals using texts at appropriate levels. A common curriculum is necessary and worthy, but expecting all students to successfully accomplish the same tasks using the same materials with the same level of support is unrealistic. Students come to us with a wide range of strengths and capabilities, so curriculum adjustments will be necessary to acknowledge these differences and provide the necessary modifications and supports.

If the intent of RTI is to ensure that students respond to *instruction*, we must be able to choose from a variety of well-designed approaches with the necessary resources and supportive professional development. As Dorn, French, and Jones (1998) emphasize, "A balanced reading program includes a range of literacy activities, carefully selected materials for each activity, and a responsive teacher who knows how to structure literacy interactions that move children to higher levels of understanding" (29). This should be the guiding principle of tier 1 instruction.

Differentiated Instruction and Supplementary Resources

Differentiated instruction is the heart and soul of tier 1, a teaching model necessitated by the wide reading range represented in each classroom. Wormeli (2006) defines differentiation as "doing what's fair" (3), while Tomlinson (2008) refers to "student-aware teaching" that is "guided by the premise that schools should maximize student potential, not simply bring students to an externally established norm on a test" (27). Differentiation acknowledges that fair is not equal and equal is not fair (Diller 2007, as quoted from Judy Wallis).

Differentiated instruction first requires that we understand how our students think and learn. It's important to gather informal data before formal assessment begins as we build a foundation for instruction. For example, we can teach students to self-select appropriate texts, engage students in reading independently, or set up partner reading for young children. We can use read-alouds to demonstrate key strategies that students can transfer to their own reading. Differentiation is feasible only if we know our students' interests, attitudes, and understandings about literacy and "their strengths and their ability to use fix-up strategies to solve reading problems" (Robb 2008, 38). Without these insights, we are reduced to guesswork or what others tell us to do.

We can differentiate content, process, or product (Tomlinson 1999). We can adjust content by increasing or decreasing the complexity or length of a task or level of the material. These adjustments *change the playing field*. We can adjust the process with physical, environmental, or instructional changes, such as spacing learning over brief sequential segments, reviewing the material more frequently, using varied seating, recording lessons, assessing students orally, or adjusting pacing to spend additional time with some students for higher levels of support. These adjustments *level the playing field*. We can adjust the product by allowing students to demonstrate their learning in different ways.

*D*ifferentiated instruction is the heart and soul of tier 1.

Effective teachers acknowledge that differentiated teaching requires differentiated texts, tasks, and materials. Resources that supplement grade-level programs are essential since there is no better way to "create" struggling readers than to give them texts they cannot read. Well-stocked, organized, classroom reading libraries make it easy to incorporate read-aloud and shared-reading activities for homogeneous and heterogeneous small-group instruction. Robb (2008) suggests that we can differentiate by providing texts on a common topic at varying levels of difficulty. We can then use read-aloud or shared reading to introduce a common skill or strategy, highlight key concepts or vocabulary, and initiate teacher- or peer-supported small-group and independent experiences.

Basal publishers have attempted to build in differentiation by offering programs below-, on-, and above-grade-level readers. Unfortunately, a closer inspection raises red flags. First, the print is often hard to read and photographs and illustrations are often of poor quality. Second, reading ability is grossly overestimated; the below-grade-level texts are still far too difficult for most struggling readers. Worse, they are simply "minibasals" in disguise.

Schools need a schoolwide book room where high-quality titles are constantly added. A well-stocked book room includes small text sets, collections of mixed-level texts on various topics, and read-aloud texts to initiate topics and instructional activities. These texts should come from a number of publishers, with at least 50 to 60 percent nonfiction related to the various content areas. Resources should be organized and labeled for easy access (Diller 2008). Leveled sets can be stored in plastic baggies labeled with key information such as "narrative" or "expository," and sets at the same level or on the same topic can be stored in labeled tubs. Remember that reading levels are flexible, subjective guidelines; we must also take student interest and background knowledge and text features into account.

Differentiation also requires adjusting the daily schedule to accommodate these experiences. Many schools refer to this daily time for small-group instruction as "sacred time." This thirty-minute block is reserved exclusively for small-group reading using texts at appropriate levels. Sacred time gives these experiences a place of honor in the day so that they are prioritized. Students are not pulled out for any reason, and professional support can be offered to individual teachers. These experiences increase *our* ability to differentiate for *our* students rather than to relinquish responsibility to others. These are not cross-grade ability groups that further segregate and isolate students. They reflect our commitment to build time into the day for intensive student-centered learning.

An important feature of differentiation is to begin with the end in mind (Covey 2004). Instruction begins with a destination, so that we always know whether we're moving in the right direction. Our destination or goal for learners is drawn from careful analysis of all assessment data and our observations of students' performances. A concrete tool toward that end is to create a *focus card*, or an index card with the purpose for reading recorded in writing (as a question). The card is then placed in clear view next to each child's copy of the book to guide the reading. This helps students keep a purpose in mind and provides a way to record relevant words, page numbers, or key points.

Wiggins and McTighe (2006) emphasize beginning with the end in mind in the context of reading using a three-step "backward design." First, identify what you want to accomplish (final destination). Then, determine what evidence (rubrics or evaluation criteria, for example) will demonstrate that your goal has been met. Finally, plan the experiences and activities you will use to achieve the goal (instructional differentiation).

Differentiation is synonymous with *responsive teaching*, in which we pay close attention to students. This cannot be scripted; our teaching changes with the changing needs of students. As we observe students engaged in various learning experiences, we redefine our thinking. Debbie Miller (2002) says, "I never know when a child or a colleague will cause me to think about things in new ways, lead me in new directions, and redefine my old thinking" (14). Teachers who differentiate recognize that the best lesson plan is the student sitting in front of them. Teachers who have a death grip on the teacher's guide invariably miss these "living" signs and markers along the way.

Differentiation is the result of a wide range of instructional opportunities that do not rely too heavily on whole-group activities. The most effective schools use more small-group experiences (Taylor et al. 2002) to reinforce and extend the understanding of *all* students. Differentiation means making spur-of-the-moment adjustments in instruction, settings, texts, or tasks to guarantee success. Its means acknowledging strengths and weaknesses with a large toolbox of varied instructional strategies. Differentiation means that we are willing to *do what's fair* by making our teaching more *student-aware*.

Targeted, More Intense Instructional Support

The third tier 1 "instructional ring" accelerates learning by offering targeted instruction for more intensive support. In some cases, this alleviates the need for higher-tier intervention. If students receive tier 2 or 3 support, it is designed to multiply these instructional experiences. We must ensure that sup-

I never know when a child or a colleague will cause me to think about things in new ways, lead me in new directions, and redefine my old thinking (Miller 2002).

port at other tiers remains *in addition to* rather than *instead of* the support we offer at tier 1.

Targeted tier 1 support always occurs in small groups or one-on-one. Group size should never exceed five, although three or fewer students may be preferable. We increase instructional intensity by decreasing group size or increasing frequency or duration. We also increase intensity by providing more feedback, guidance, and scaffolded support (modeling, for example). In fact, some say that good teaching falls into three basic phases: demonstrations, coaching, and supported practice. Teachers who move their instruction through these phases are able to individualize instruction every day quite naturally and easily.

Targeted instruction at tier 1 is manageable (since few students need it). These instructional experiences center around high-quality resources (meaningful texts rather than the typical decodable texts in many packaged intervention programs) and reflect reading level rather than grade level. A steady diet of dull, meaningless texts will exacerbate the problem, so our first goal is to increase the opportunities for engaging, high-success reading. Every classroom experience can inform the selection and design of these activities. *You* are the most powerful teacher's guide if you are willing to use your knowledge about literacy and students to drive your teaching.

Taberski's umbrella of comprehension offers an essential instructional design for these experiences (2009). Making meaning should be the goal of every instructional action and every activity in which we engage students. Building vocabulary, fluency, background knowledge, and students' use of metacognitive strategies all fall under the umbrella of teaching students to comprehend. Similarly, Rasinski, Rupley, and Nichols (2008) suggest blending phonics and fluency in poetry. Embedding skills in pleasurable, meaningful texts keeps the focus on more than surface features of print and points our instructional compass to comprehension at all times.

Targeted instruction is designed to teach struggling readers the same key strategies used by proficient readers. Activities focus on whole-to-part instruction using meaningful texts and tasks to build "a literacy of thoughtfulness that includes conscious, effective strategy use" (Hoyt 2005). If we focus on discrete isolated concepts without allowing students to apply this learning in real contexts, transfer is unlikely. Small-group guided reading is an excellent way to teach these more focused skills or strategies using meaningful texts that match children's needs.

Content-area instruction is an important time to teach critical literacy strategies with expository texts. Independent reading of easy, self-selected

You are the most powerful teacher's guide if you are willing to use your knowledge about literacy and students to drive your teaching.

texts is also a rich opportunity for teaching. One-to-one conferences allow us to use student-selected texts to teach important learning within a pleasurable assessment/instructional routine (Routman 2003). These informal ten-minute discussions create more student-centered experiences. Occasionally, we can make time for deeper discussions to celebrate "the luscious feeling of endless time" (Miller 2008, 106).

We must also collaborate with those providing tier 2 and 3 intervention so that all levels of support are coordinated. This does not mean that we replicate these support experiences, but pull them from a common strategy toolbox. In this way students don't become confused, and we can reinforce learning, highlight related topics of interest, and teach instructional strategies in various contexts. This is especially important for struggling readers since collaboration will enhance each learning opportunity.

It isn't hard to find time in the day for targeted instruction if we examine our daily activities and eliminate those that don't advance learning. Do we want to assign worksheet pages or work with small groups of students? Do we want to grade papers while students work independently, or use these moments for more intensive instruction? Seizing these opportunities requires determination and discrimination about what is really important. These teachable moments are ours for the taking. *Use 'em or lose 'em.*

Continuous Assessment to Inform and Support Instruction

Most RTI assessment involves universal screening and progress monitoring, key features of tier 1. An entire school population is screened at three intervals to determine which students will navigate grade-level curriculum successfully. Progress monitoring occurs during interventions to determine whether the instruction is successful and to become the basis for adjustments if it is not. These assessment features are discussed in detail in Chapter 6. One note of caution here, however, is that progress monitoring often focuses more on surface features—fluency and accuracy—rather than on meaning. We must balance progress monitoring tools with those that focus on meaning.

RTI emphasizes that screening and progress monitoring make teaching more instructionally responsive. But do these assessments alone allow us to meet this goal? If we limit our assessment to the data collection of RTI, we may miss essential options. Instructional responsiveness requires us to draw from a wide range of sources, particularly those rooted in active engagement in learning. We cannot exclude the rich informal assessment that rises from observing

YELLOW

/t isn't hard to find time in the day for targeted instruction if we examine our daily activities and eliminate those that don't advance learning.

students engaged in learning. While I doubt this is the intention, the time and energy required to learn and implement RTI data collection carry the risk that other critical assessments will be eliminated. The added demands of RTI data collection may cause teachers to abandon other more important assessment features in exasperation.

Assessment and instruction are inseparable. Effective assessment is on-going, rising from instruction to generate new assessment/instructional opportunities. Grading is a common concern; many teachers expect every assessment to lead to a grade. They are hesitant to give up worksheets or end-of-chapter questions. They recognize the limited value of these things but worry about having enough grades to fill a grade book. Hence a conundrum: assessment informs and supports the grades we give, but it is not grading.

Effective assessment includes evaluation. Assessment is the process of gathering information from a wide range of sources; evaluation is the process of placing value on that information. This may lead to a grade, but it also reflects analysis of data for deeper levels of understanding, enabling us to make informed decisions that lead to new instruction (Caldwell 2002). Expert teachers view assessment as a natural part of the day and take advantage of any opportunity to gather assessment data to inform their teaching. They use summative assessment to evaluate learning with an end score after the fact, but emphasize formative assessment that can highlight learning needs and improve instruction. They watch for the signs of success as well as confusion and use this information to enhance their teaching.

A key assessment procedure embedded in learning is to check for understanding. Fisher and Frey (2007) recommend we do this every fifteen minutes to reinforce current learning, correct misconceptions, or enhance subsequent learning. Ongoing checkpoints allow us to demonstrate how to monitor understanding as we give students a model for good study skills. Checking for understanding is a formative assessment since it occurs during instruction or active engagement in a learning activity.

Assessment can also help us select appropriate texts for instructional purposes or guide students as they look for independent texts on topics of interest. I find that the most common scores teachers recite when I inquire about reading level—AR (Accelerated Reader) levels or DIBELS (Dynamic Indicators of Basic Early Literacy Skills)—are least informative. Neither offers the insight I need to select appropriate texts or instructional strategies nor do they tap students' understanding of their reading.

The most effective way to analyze students' accuracy and strategy use is simply to listen to them read. Expert teachers know that the only way to understand strategies student are using (or confusing) is to listen to them read

*E*xpert teachers view assessment as a natural part of the day.

one-on-one, thus opening a "window on the reading process" (Goodman 1969, 123). This may occur informally as we move about the room with a clipboard, listening to students read and taking notes that provide valuable information we can revisit over time.

We can also take running records to analyze more closely the strategies students use or fail to use in the context of reading—cueing systems (structural and visual), cross-checking one strategy against another, self-monitoring strategies such as rereading or self-correction. This information lets us identify their independent, instructional, and frustration reading levels and select texts more effectively. Matching texts and students requires being knowledgeable about both. This is far more effective than depending on publishers to tell us which texts match students they don't even know.

DETERMINING STUDENTS' READING LEVELS

Several useful guidelines can help determine reading level. The most common is that used in Reading Recovery (Clay 1985), in which independent texts are those read with 95 to 100 percent accuracy and instructional texts are those read with 90 to 94 percent accuracy. These guidelines are lower than those suggested by Betts (1946), who cites independent as 99 or 100 percent and instructional as 95 to 98 percent. Powell and Dunkeld (1971) use "floating" criteria according to grade level—independent reading is 94 percent or greater accuracy in kindergarten to grade 2, 96 percent or greater accuracy in grades 3 through 5, and 97 percent or greater accuracy in grade 6 and above.

These are all useful systems, although schools should use one consistently so each teacher has a common view. Remember too that recommendations are guidelines rather than hard-and-fast rules. Also, they deal only with accuracy; we need to consider factors such as meaningful substitutions, familiarity with text features, prior knowledge, whether the material is narrative or expository, and comprehension. Simply being handed a list of scores, though common practice, has limited value in making these decisions.

These levels must be used flexibly for instructional purposes. The leveling systems in packaged programs are very subjective and often overestimate reading level. Select texts based on the context as well, using a range of text levels rather than relying on a single number or letter designation. For example, easier texts are recommended to introduce a new skill, strategy, or concept or when the goal is to reinforce learning. A factual selection also warrants an easier reading level than narrative texts.

Also, "the size of the 'leaps' children make has limits" (Cunningham and Allington 2006). A fourth grader at an instructional reading level of 2.5 may be able to read a text ranked 3.0, but it is not realistic to ask that student to read a text ranked 4.5. Necessarily, the intervals between levels for very young children are narrow to reflect their emerging reading ability. As children move through the grades, the intervals widen. In estimating reading level, it is always preferable to err on the easy side. Independent texts will reinforce a child's growing literacy knowledge, while frustrating texts do little more than create unpleasant reading experiences that intensify a student's struggle.

Leveling systems of any kind are for teachers, not students. Organizing a school or classroom library by level or labeling texts using level designation, whether coded or not, is strongly discouraged. Consider your personal experiences at the public library. I've never been told I could only peruse books in the "fifty-nine-year-old section." If we teach students to self-select texts from a variety of options on interesting topics, we can trust them to make good choices. These selections then support students' development as independent readers (Allison 2007). Of course, this assumes that students have access to quality texts in a well-stocked classroom library.

Many schools use schoolwide professional collaboration to examine text levels in meaningful ways. One such approach is an "assessment wall" that visually explores growth in and across grades (Dorn and Soffos 2001). The (anonymous and coded) reading levels of students are displayed on the wall. Teachers together periodically reevaluate students' levels and move the cards accordingly. This encourages professional dialogue that helps to identify students who may need support.

Ongoing observation of students' literacy is a very effective informal assessment. It is important to use a recording system that allows all this information to be reviewed during the year. A simple procedure is to create a file folder for each child. Each week, take a sheet of adhesive address labels and write each child's name at the top of a label. During the week, record anecdotal notes on the address label with the child's name. After you record your notes, date the label and transfer it to the child's file folder. You can quickly see who has not been assessed that week by looking at the remaining empty labels. The weekly notations in each file rapidly grow over time.

When we treat assessment and instruction as inseparable components of tier 1 intervention, we can offer assessment in any and all "instructional rings." While screening and progress monitoring both have a role in assessment, they are only two components. Other forms of assessment are equally important and should become a natural part of the learning day. Ongoing assessment helps us teach more responsively and intentionally—a far more important and informative practice than simply collecting numerical data.

Connecting the Instructional Rings: A Framework for Teaching

Once each instructional ring is in place, the gradual release of responsibility model gives us a framework for learning (Pearson and Gallagher 1983). Routman (2003) refers to this as the optimal learning model across the curriculum. The term "across the curriculum" is an important perspective—the framework supports every aspect of the learning day and emphasizes teacher-supported learning, which is too often deemphasized or even missing.

New learning requires high support before students assume independence. Thus, the framework begins with high levels of modeling and teacher support; the teacher then gradually relinquishes support in a series of shared and guided demonstrations until students assume full control (independent learning). Independence is a gradual process that requires ample scaffolding and support that is slowly withdrawn (see Figure 3.2). We can do a good job of teaching, but jeopardize that work by leaping too quickly to test independence. If we linger longer in the middle stage, and offer more support and coaching, we can increase the expertise necessary for independence.

Of course, at higher tiers of RTI, longer and more intensive periods of teacher support are needed. We can illustrate this by changing the shape of the tiered triangle and superimposing it over the release-of-responsibility rectangle (see Figure 3.3). Higher tiers of intensity require more modeled, shared, and guided experiences, while tier 1 intervention stretches across every component of learning.

Figure 3.2 The Gradual Release of Responsibility (Pearson and Gallagher 1983)

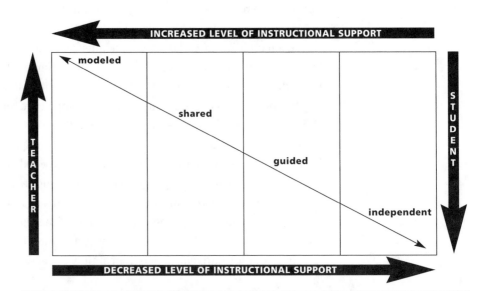

Figure 3.3 Integrating the RTI Framework and Gradual Release Model

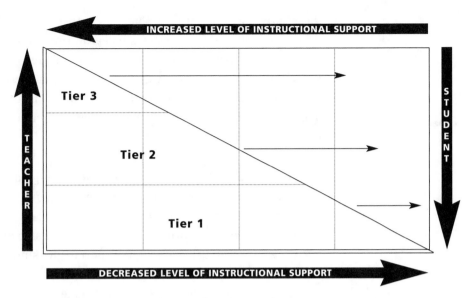

The gradual release of responsibility includes four key stages: (1) full teacher control through modeling (*I do as you watch*); teacher-supported student engagement in (2) shared and (3) guided demonstration (*we do together*); and (4) full student control during independent application (*you do*). This transfer of responsibility allows us to "give students supports that they can hold on to as they take the lead—not just push them onto the path and hope they find their way" (Fisher and Frey 2008a, 33).

MODELING Teacher modeling has a significant impact on learning. Fisher, Frey, and Lapp (2008a) state, "Modeling provides students with pictorial, process, and linguistic examples, which serve as the cognitive hooks on which they can hang new information" (3). These demonstrations allow us to assume full control, publicly demonstrating a cognitive process before we ask students to undertake it on their own. Students watch and listen as we provide an explicit model as they mentally mirror this thinking. We think aloud, revealing what goes on in our mind as we complete a particular task, giving students a model for how an expert approaches and solves a problem. This paves the way for students to apply this learning later. If we neglect this important stage, it impacts everything that follows.

SHARED DEMONSTRATION Holdaway (1979, 1983) first described shared reading using a Big Book to model reading as young children watched. Shared demonstrations blend teacher modeling with student engagement in a meaningful activity to help students apply learning in authentic contexts. Thus, we continue to model thinking while we begin to increase student engagement in these early stages of learning. Shared demonstrations occur in a variety of instructional settings: whole class, small group, or one-on-one. Shared reading is an excellent way to model and teach comprehension, vocabulary, text structures, and text features at any grade level. Routman describes Holdaway's influence on her thinking: "I carry the model in my head, and I try to employ it in every teaching situation. When my teaching breaks down, I go back to the model" (1991, 9).

GUIDED PRACTICE In guided practice, support is gradually withdrawn as students engage in the learning activity more directly, moving toward independence. There is still give-and-take between teacher and student, but students assume more control. During guided practice, we step in and out of the learning process, providing just enough support to give students room to control their own learning and achieve increasing independence. Guided reading is an engaging small-group activity blending teacher support and student independent application. Miller (2002) refers to students' "having at it" (10) by reading a carefully selected text as the teacher reinforces strategies they know how to use, prompts them to use less familiar strategies, provide scaffolds if necessary, and coaches them to apply new learning. This interweaving of independence and support allows expert teachers to make on-the-spot adjustments.

INDEPENDENT APPLICATION During independent application, students, unsupported, apply what they have learned. Students are often pushed into this stage too quickly or, conversely, are never given the opportunities to put new learning into practice. Independent learning is not *new* learning, but learning that is within students' control, that they can apply successfully on their own. We are still available to offer support and feedback as needed, but we have given them the tools they need to assume control. We may provide supportive reminders such as strategy bookmarks or evaluation criteria such as rubrics or checklists. Remember that independent learning is just that—independent. If students cannot eventually control their own learning, we have skipped important stages in instruction. And if that is the case, any learning they may demonstrate is fleeting at best.

> *I*ndependent learning is not *new* learning, but learning that is within students' control.

PEER COLLABORATION Peer collaboration has been suggested as an important component of the gradual release of responsibility model (Fisher, Frey, and Lapp 2008a, b; Fisher and Frey 2008a, b). This offers an interim step before students work on their own. This extension of shared and guided practice makes sense: teacher-supported *peer* experiences reinforce the tools and strategies needed for independence while encouraging heterogeneous learning.

Ensuring High-Quality Tier 1 Instruction, Differentiation, and Intervention

The gradual release of responsibility model emphasizes the teacher's role in the instructional process. Effective teachers do not *tell* students what to do; rather, the instructional process, or *how* we teach, is as important as *what* we teach. The learning process should actively engage both teachers and students.

This model also highlights research on the power of language and how the words we choose matter. Johnston (2004) states, "Talk is the central tool of [teachers'] trade. With it they mediate children's activity and experience, and help them make sense of learning, literacy, life, and themselves" (4). Our words allow us to support students as they make sense of learning; what we say and how we say it influences their thinking. By being "thoughtfully explicit" in the language we use and prompting students to take this language as their own, we help them make sense of their world and of the process of learning. This cannot be scripted because it rises from our instructional experiences.

Classroom teachers are essential to the success of tier 1—the tier that impacts every moment of the day. This means that we must pay close attention to the characteristics of effective teaching (Pressley et al. 1998; Allington and Johnston 2000). Allington (2002) identifies "six Ts" of effective literacy instruction:

Allington's Six Ts

1. *Time*. Exemplary teachers fill the day with reading and writing rather than "stuff." ("Stuff" is everything that steals time from real reading and writing, such as worksheets, computerized tests, and contrived after-reading tasks.) In the most effective classrooms, students are engaged in authentic reading and writing at least 50 percent of the day, yet students in less effective classrooms read as little as 10 percent of the day, or less than thirty minutes! If it takes twenty minutes to build students' prior knowledge when three minutes is adequate, this is time not spent reading. Expert teachers immerse students in reading to ensure that they read a substantial portion of the day.

2. *Texts.* Students will become proficient readers only if they have many opportunities to read texts they can read with understanding. Successful reading is reading with *accuracy, fluency,* and *comprehension*. Expert teachers refuse to distribute identical grade-level material to everyone in the class, since few things are less scientific than a one-size-fits-all approach. Effective classrooms include small-group and independent reading experiences using high-success texts. There is no better way to create struggling readers than to provide a steady diet of texts they find impossible to read.

3. **Teach.** Exemplary teachers engage students in active instruction most of the day. They turn away from "assign and assess," where students merely complete activities for a grade. Active instruction means teachers explicitly model and demonstrate cognitive strategies used by successful readers. They think aloud in authentic contexts so students can understand this thinking before applying it independently. They move from teacher-supported to independent learning as they gradually relinquish control. Expert teachers avoid worksheets or end-of-the-story questions, opting instead for active learning.

4. **Talk.** The quality of classroom talk is very different in exemplary classrooms. Expert teachers use talk purposefully to engage students in posing and solving problems. This occurs across the curriculum in teacher-to-student or student-to-student interactions with talk that is more conversational than interrogational. Students engage in meaningful discussions that revolve around thought-provoking questions, often ones they have raised themselves. This kind of talk cannot be scripted in a teacher's guide of rigid questions with yes-no answers or facts-in-the-text responses. It comes from insightful teachers who pay attention to students' needs as they interact in meaningful literacy events.

5. **Tasks.** Tasks in exemplary classrooms tend to be longer and more elaborate, often with research projects centered on topics of interest across the curriculum. Students are less likely to complete worksheets and more likely to engage in activities that use varied research and study tools to reach deeper levels of understanding. Expert teachers take personal interests into account and use a range of texts to match the needs of students. These experiences are hard to rank from best to worst (unlike worksheets, where each is the same). Student responses are not viewed as better or worse but different, and learning is emphasized over ranking. This leads to more student engagement and less off-task behavior.

6. **Test.** Expert teachers view grading as a process of effort and improvement. (In traditional grading, some students don't have to work very hard, while others find that hard work rarely leads to improved grades.) Expert teachers use rubrics to establish evaluation criteria and explain them to their students in detail. They place responsibility for grades on students and are always aware where students begin or how much they grow over time. Parents don't complain about this type of grading, because it is carefully explained and documented; they understand that everyone has an equal chance for a grade based on effort and improvement. Expert teachers rarely succumb to a "test prep mentality"; they know that good teaching leads to higher grades.

GREEN

Steps You Can Take Toward a Differentiated Classroom

Emphasizing expert teaching over programs requires a shift in thinking and on-going schoolwide support that is not always available. The most highly qualified teachers are frequently assigned to higher tiers of intervention, but this does not alleviate the need for expert teaching at tier 1. Nor is expert teaching limited to literacy; it extends to all we do in a day. Expert teachers consistently apply the same guidelines, regardless of the clock on the wall, and insist on active engagement in high-quality texts and tasks all day long.

*E*xpert teachers insist on active engagement in high-quality texts and tasks all day long.

Differentiated professional development is a key part of this process. Long-term support revolves around practices, not packages, as we learn to think more critically and reflectively about our instruction. Many schools have reading coaches, but fail to take advantage of this support system. Walpole and Blamey (2008) emphasize the dual role of coaches and their need to devote as much time to the *mentor* role (supporting teachers) as to the *director* role (guiding the literacy program). Many reading specialists work with students all day, when they would have more impact mentoring classroom teachers in the use of instructional techniques—assuming they are themselves expert teachers. We must promote professional conversations or "teacher talk" to drive and sustain change—or suffer the consequences of superficial change (Routman 2002).

> Exemplary teaching is responsive to children's needs, not regurgitation of a common script. In the end, it will become clearer that there are no "proven programs," just schools where we find more expert teachers—teachers who need no script to tell them what to do.
>
> —*Richard Allington*

Use the "backward design" to create your own literacy program. By identifying what you value, you can embed those values into your teaching every day. Your classroom reflects what matters to you. Substantially increase the amount of reading your students do, using books they *can* read. Having thirty students read the same anthology sends a message that you do not value differentiation. If you do not create an independent-reading library, you are dismissing reading as irrelevant. Does our day really reflect your values? Once you identify what you value, build your schedule around these things; don't sacrifice them to politics or expediency. Make room for what you hold dear, even if you have to adjust the clock. Those things that matter most should not be the first to go, no matter how busy you are. Broaden your view of literacy so that it is not confined to the hours between 8 and 10 A.M. You want to show students that they can apply a good reading strategy during social studies or read about science in reading workshop. Spread rich literacy instructional experiences across the school day and then send these literacy events home with students to reinforce and celebrate that learning!

Now that your day reflects what you value, create a learning environment that supports differentiation. Build a reading library brimming with a wide variety of texts at each child's independent reading level and organize them by topic or theme in labeled bins. Schedule daily heterogeneous and homogeneous small-group activities. Use wall space wisely: have your students create "walls that teach" as resources for learning. Display evidence of enthusiastic learning: Favorite Facts About Seals, Books Fifth Graders Love, Words First Graders Can Read. Create reading "advertisements" in the form of book baskets that travel to other classrooms in search of new readers.

Now that you have created a foundation for expert teaching, insist on maintaining responsibility for your own students for tier 1 instruction. Deep understanding of students' needs comes from spending all day with them. Do you want another classroom teacher to provide thirty minutes of instruction down the hall, or do you want to embed your own expertise into the six hours of instruction you provide every day, five days a week? Be responsible for your own teaching within tier 1. Doing the right thing means being willing to make the hard choices even when it's not the easy road.

Take advantage of each precious moment by moving around the room as students work independently. Expert teachers are never still; we watch our students as they write, listen to students read, and hold conferences that both teach and inform instruction. With every tick of the clock, another opportunity for instruction is lost forever. We are flooded with an unending amount of "stuff" that wastes time we could spend observing or interacting with students in meaningful literacy events. Make responsible choices about what you allow to creep into your schedule and fill every day with valuable learning opportunities. That's a respectable habit with a big payoff.

Tier 1 instruction is the most critical ingredient in the RTI mix. Unless we are willing to expend the energy and thought that will make our instruction exemplary, we will never be able to provide the extra support our students need and deserve. If tier 1 instruction doesn't reach every student, regardless of reading level, more students will need tier 2 and 3 intervention. This will overtax the intervention system and penalize students for our failure to provide high-

*W*ith every tick of the clock, another opportunity for instruction is lost forever.

quality instruction from the bottom up. We cannot make differentiation a sometimes thing (Ankrum and Bean 2007); it requires a conscious and purposeful daily effort.

The International Reading Association (2000) puts expert tier 1 instruction and differentiation into perspective by emphasizing that "making a difference means making it different . . . Programs that center on one part of the literacy equation at the expense of others train readers who may be unable to understand or enjoy what they read" (2). Tier 1 incorporates a wide variety of instructional strategies, resources, and approaches that also acknowledge the motivation that gives students the impetus to learn to read in the first place. Tier 1 instruction never loses sight of the critical role of comprehension, viewing reading as a fruitless effort unless students can do so with understanding.

Expert tier 1 teachers assume a central role in the design and implementation of their own instruction, even if it means bucking the system by "going against the grain" (Allington 2002), and effective schools support this role. As expert teachers, we must resist following scripts, opting to promote deeper understanding along with our students' growing knowledge—and our growing knowledge of them. Simply meeting the requirements of a packaged program puts us back in a position of juggling elephants—an impossible task that hurts our students immeasurably. Unless we are willing to fight for the right to use our own expertise above all that is "stuffed" into our day, we will not have the time, energy, or desire left to "go against the grain." Expert teaching must be nurtured—by districts, by schools, and by our own expectations.

What you do matters when you make every day matter for your students.

Yes, tier 1 is in *your* capable hands, my friends. *You*—and you alone—are the ringmaster who will make a difference for readers who struggle. What you do matters when you make every day matter for your students, regardless of demands and politics that may impede your efforts. You add the talented human touch we are dangerously close to losing. You, and you alone, can bring RTI to life.

The three-ring circus metaphor takes on new meaning when we set our sights on expert teaching and a passionate search for high-quality literacy performances. Let the show begin!

CHAPTER 4

Tier 2 Intervention: Establishing a Coordinated Continuum of Support

A green thumb is nothing more than hard work and the desire to make things grow.

—*Albert E. Tuttle*

In Jon J. Muth's picture book *The Three Questions*, we learn about a boy named Nikolai who wants to be a good person and do the right thing, but first he must answer three questions: *When is the best time to do things? Who is the most important one? What is the right thing to do?* Convinced that only wise old Leo the Turtle can answer his questions, he sets out on a journey. While Nikolai awaits his answer, he helps Leo dig his garden and saves a Panda and her child from the storm. In the end, Nikolai's questions are answered: the most important time is now; the most important person is the one you are with; the most important thing to do is good for the one you are with (Muth 2002).

Nikolai's answers to what is important in this world can guide our inquiry into what is important in meeting the needs of struggling readers. *The most important time is now. The most important one is each individual child. The most important thing to do is good for that child.* Expert teachers make daily on-the-spot decisions about what is the right thing to do for each child now. *This* is what is most important at tier 2—or any tier.

As we explored in the previous chapter, we can meet the needs of 80 percent of students at tier 1 through high-quality, differentiated instruction, but even that is insufficient for about 20 percent of our students. Tier 2 offers an instructional safety net that works in concert with tier 1 to add both time and instructional intensity into the day. This combined effort increases the likelihood that students will be successful within a general literacy setting.

Codie's Story

To underscore the role of tier 2 and its connection with tier 1, it is helpful to consider students with unique needs that require differentiated approaches. We'll begin with a first grader, Codie, to demonstrate how Nikolai's questions are answered from an instructional perspective (all names are pseudonyms but stories are based on actual students).

Codie attended kindergarten and the first half of first grade in another state. School records showed that he lagged behind his peers from the beginning and parent information revealed that he had experienced numerous ear infections prior to entering school. His previous teachers had noted only that he was unable to discriminate between sounds, had difficulty learning the alphabet, and was not developing a reading or writing sight vocabulary. Unfortunately, no steps had been taken to address these concerns or offer instructional support.

By the time Codie entered his new school in the middle of first grade, he was significantly behind his peers. His first grade teacher confirmed that Codie had difficulty discriminating sounds, but also noted that he enthusiastically joined in during whole-class shared-reading experiences. Assessment showed that he knew only three sight words: *the, a, I.* He could identify all letters of the alphabet by name and knew most of the sounds, but he had difficulty blending known sounds together to form words.

A team including the administrator, reading specialist, first grade teacher, school nurse and speech therapist decided Codie needed tier 2 support. Since the tier 1 teacher had twenty-eight students, the reading specialist would offer tier 2 support in a one-on-one intensive approach. Twenty-minute daily sessions were scheduled and he was placed in speech therapy. Codie's progress was monitored in each setting for one month.

Three instructional goals were established: developing Codie's sight word knowledge, understanding of sound patterns, and use of early reading strategies. Predictable, repetitive texts for beginning readers were carefully selected so that these goals could be taught within authentic contexts. The schoolwide book room had a large collection of high-quality early readers that could be used for guided reading experiences.

The reading specialist and tier 1 teacher also collaborated to create an instructional cycle that could be used in *both* settings. The tier 1 teacher observed guided reading sessions conducted by the reading specialist to provide her with a knowledge base for teachers to use a common approach. The reading specialist provided a mini-word wall for Codie to house sight words using a file folder. A reading bookmark was also provided to highlight the early reading strategies being promoted. The tier 1 teacher liked these strategies so much that she provided them for several students.

Each session began with a one-minute writing spree to reinforce Codie's sight words. He wrote a word on a dry-erase board and it was erased and rewritten several times. Each text was selected to reinforce words and patterns for repeated exposure. Codie framed high-frequency words between his index fingers and often generated new words using a common pattern (*like, hike, bike, Mike*). This learning was highlighted in a make-and-break activity with magnetic letters.

After each reading, Codie generated a sentence about the book he had read to reinforce words and patterns in the text. This interactive writing activity engaged Codie and the teacher as the pen changed hands back and forth. The make-and-break magnetic letter activity was used for selected words and sound boxes (Elkonin) were initiated. Using this strategy, the teacher drew a box with a section for each sounded. Codie pushed a token as he said the word slowly to identify and record the letter in the appropriate box. This helped Codie to focus on sounds and patterns in simple CVC words (*can*).

To reinforce words across both tiers, teachers created a strategy called "pocket words." Each day, Codie recorded any new words on a small strip of paper that he placed in his pocket. When he returned to the classroom, his teacher asked, "What are your pocket words?" Codie removed the paper with a grin and read the words as she recorded them on a list. He repeated this activity in tier 2 so common words could be reinforced across tiers. This wonderful activity always brought a smile to Codie's face.

A meeting was held at the end of one month to determine Codie's progress. Each teacher completed an initial assessment based on a sight word list and a running record. Assessments demonstrated that Codie had made progress but that continued accelerated support was warranted. The tier 1 teacher reduced Codie's guided reading group to three and teachers met regularly to discuss his progress. After six weeks, Codie received a second round of tier 2 to maintain the momentum as teachers continued to collaborate.

Codie's experience illustrates the interactive relationship of tier 1 and 2. Codie received a double dose of instruction since tier 2 occurred beyond the time designated for classroom reading instruction. The tier 1 teacher was involved in Codie's complete learning program and she learned new strategies that would benefit Codie as well as other students. She integrated shared reading and interactive writing into her reading program and incorporated framing words, mini-word wall and reading bookmarks. She recorded and read nursery rhymes with students daily to support Codie's development of sounds in a pleasurable activity. Both the tier 1 and tier 2 teachers had common language with a mutually supportive and consistent approach.

Every decision was based on Codie's needs and the results were positive. After a second round of tier 2 and continued collaboration with the tier 1 teacher, Codie returned to the general education setting on a full-time basis. The reading specialist monitored his progress for four weeks and visited with the teacher regularly to ensure that there was not a progress slide. A combination of the ongoing support from the tier 2 teacher and the tier 1 teacher's willingness to integrate new instructional approaches into the day ensured Codie's continued development. By the time he entered grade 2, the gap was closed and Codie flourished.

Broadening the Instructional Safety Net

*F*ailing to support our teachers is the same as failing to support our students. This makes students pay for our limitations on both counts.

Codie's story illustrates how a tiered framework is adjusted to meet the needs of students. Notice that tier 2 extended rather than replaced tier 1 and adjustments were made in tier 1 to ensure coordination of high-quality instruction in both settings. In some cases, failure to respond is an issue of teacher expertise so professional support must be offered. Even Codie's dedicated teacher was given access to these professional learning opportunities. We can only explore RTI from all angles if we reexamine both teaching *and* learning. Failing to support our teachers is the same as failing to support our students. This makes students pay for our limitations on both counts.

Tier 2, often described as strategic supplemental intervention, is thirty minutes of daily support *in addition to* tier 1 instruction. Percentages cited vary, but the common view is that tier 2 support is needed only by 10 to 15 percent of students. Intervention of tier 2 will *not* occur during time designated for tier 1 instruction or students will not receive the additional help they need—*more time, more instruction, more intensity*. This entails creative scheduling to make sure students don't miss popular activities like recess, art, music, or physical education so that students are not penalized.

Tier 2 is a temporary support system; the goal is to provide accelerated learning that enables students to return to the regular classroom as soon as possible. While a schedule is typically established for entering or exiting tier 2, this is always based on student need. Codie was given immediate entry into tier 2 so that teachers could provide the specific instruction he needed at that time. The combined effort of tier 1 and 2 teachers created a spirit of *shared responsibility*—instructional collaboration and coordination between tiers.

Tier 2 intervention occurs in small-group, homogeneous instructional settings—students who have similar learning needs. Decreasing the size of the group increases the instructional intensity as well as the likelihood that the teacher can provide the right support at the right time. Groups are three to five students, but limiting the size to three students accelerates progress. As the needs of the group members increase, group size decreases. This flexibility is feasible, since relatively few students need tier 2 support. Of course, the importance of group size pales in comparison to the role of high-quality instruction. The number of students in each group is irrelevant if the quality of instruction is low.

Four essential features are integral to tier 2 and should be emphasized as key goals (specific details will vary from school to school). I'll use Codie as an example to illustrate these features, which are addressed in more detail in the next sections.

GREEN

1. ***Supplementary resources to implement high-quality instructional strategies.*** For example, Codie's tier 2 teacher used a variety of high-quality texts that reflected his reading need and interests. His tier 1 teacher had freedom to select texts outside of the reading program that were more appropriate for Codie. The basis for selecting instructional texts can then focus on reading level over an assigned grade level.

2. ***Targeted interventions at higher levels of intensity.*** For example, Codie needed more instructional intensity. The tier 1 teacher accomplished this by decreasing the size of his guided reading group to three while the tier 2 teacher used a one-to-one approach. Intensity was also increased with more modeling, feedback, and reinforcement in both tiers.

3. ***Ongoing formal and informal assessment.*** For example, both teachers completed three weekly assessments in each setting: one-minute word recognition list, one-minute writing spree, and a running record on the current guided reading book.

This allowed them to determine whether the goals established were being met in tier 2 and then transferred to tier 1.

4. **Team decision making and collaboration.** For example, Codie's tier 1 and 2 teachers met weekly to look at combined assessments and decide on the next step. They made adjustments in the complexity of texts through this collaboration. The tier 1 teacher also observed a tier 2 lesson so that common instructional strategies could be initiated.

Supplementary Resources to Implement High-Quality Instructional Strategies

The supplementary resources of tier 2 *reinforce and extend* classroom literacy teaching and learning. My warning about prepackaged programs still holds: let's intensify support with high-quality resources and *teacher-designed* instruction aligned to each student's needs. We must do this in ways that don't just repeat tier 1 instruction that is not working for these children and modify accordingly. We have to avoid grade-level reading resources and *work more intensely* within *the child's reading level.* Viewing this second tier exclusively in terms of commercial intervention programs is sheer folly. We must learn to be good consumers by selecting the best resources available when the stakes are so high.

YELLOW

Most tier 2 students are already frustrated readers. I can't think of a better way to further frustrate children like Codie than to force them to bark at print all day. Yet, many programs do exactly that. Guided reading is a key instructional activity for tier 2 because we can promote strategies and skills using authentic contexts with texts that are carefully matched to students. Guided reading engages them in contextual reading with support, guidance, and feedback. Many programs focus tier 2 interventions on isolated skills. As a Reading Recovery teacher, I did not withhold these critical experiences until students had the "right" number of discrete skills, but integrated them into real literacy experiences.

We can also promote this learning in other meaningful activities, just as Codie's tier 1 teacher responsibly chose to do. She used the same instructional strategies during shared reading and read-aloud, allowing critical learning to revolve around rich texts. Too often skills are viewed as separate activities done outside of reading. I defy anyone to show me a skill (one worth teaching, of course) that cannot be expertly integrated into authentic reading. Further, I challenge anyone to cite any logical evidence that a worksheet is more effective than deeper engagement through a second reading of an interesting and appealing high-quality text.

The supplemental resources we select for guided reading are also worth emphasizing. Guided reading resources consist of high-quality texts, appealing texts (which can be purchased with money saved by not purchasing programs or skill-and-drill activities) that students can read with the support of the teacher. Irene Fountas and Gay Su Pinnell offer a high-quality intervention program with many resources (www.fountasandpinnell.com), and companies—such as National Geographic, Mondo Press, Wright Group, Rigby, Benchmark Education, and Scholastic—offer outstanding text options. While many companies make the mistake of adding trivial paper-pencil tasks, the overall quality is a quantum leap next to the leveled readers provided by basal publishers. Responsible schools can refuse trivial resources publishers provide and opt only for the most effective ones.

Another excellent strategy is to use students' spoken language to generate print and use these student-dictated texts as a source for guided reading. The teacher records the student's oral language in printed form. The child can then read the resulting print so that his/her personal language is used for reading. Teachers may also use student-created books as a reading activity. Skill and strategy possibilities abound in a link between oral and written language that provides a rich source for reading.

Unfortunately, many commercial intervention programs consist of decodable or controlled texts with stories devoid of meaning. Subjecting struggling readers to dull, meaningless texts does little to relieve their frustration and may even heighten it. Frankly, I find it hard to care whether *Fat Pat sat on a mat with that rat.* More to the point, our reluctant readers will not be on the edge of their seats. We must be more responsible about the texts we put in the hands of students who are not yet convinced that reading is a worthy pursuit.

Basal publishers offer on-grade-level, below-grade-level, and above-grade-level readers that emphasize common vocabulary, making this skill more important than the story line. Schools often purchase a distinct program for each tier or emphasize scripted programs, yet "nothing in the law requires them [interventions] to be scripted" (Mesmer and Mesmer 2009, 285). This makes alignment between tiers virtually impossible.

Some schools I've visited substitute computer software for expert tier 2 teachers. While this may be less expensive, it is certainly not the solution. Every avenue should be explored to put expert teachers at the top of the list of priorities. Software programs can be surprisingly costly. Imagine the financial resources at our disposal if we opt to spend available funds on people rather than "stuff." Trivial tasks, whether on screen or on paper, waste valuable time. Interventions must offer purposeful, teacher-supported instructional activities that

*I*magine the financial resources at our disposal if we opt to spend available funds on people rather than "stuff."

help students learn in engaging ways. This does not mean exercises are never part of learning, but that resources for interventions are instructionally based— real teachers working with students engaged in meaningful literacy events. Otherwise, we may as well dole out the material, turn on the computers, and go home. Quite simply, teachers are far too important to relinquish a central role in the instructional process. If student needs are our focus, interventions must be instructionally responsive.

Targeted Interventions at Higher Levels of Intensity

Tier 2 intervention provides support beyond modifications or accommodations such as altering seating arrangements or reading questions orally. Interventions focus on specific skills and strategies that address students' learning needs. These skills and strategies are emphasized in meaningful contexts where students never lose sight of the ultimate goal of enjoying and understanding interesting texts. If students struggle with phonics, instruction promotes this learning in the context of reading: phonics is still phonics but we teach students to *use* phonics rather than simply to *do* phonics. Notice that Codie's intervention incorporated word work, phonics, vocabulary, and fluency into a much loftier goal of comprehension. In fact, most special education services in the past were based on a "skills-in-isolation" approach. This may account for some students' lack of success (Bentum and Aaron 2003). Few of us learn without a rich contextual hook for that learning.

Some schools create a "site intervention library"—a "strategy in a bag." These are not packages or scripts, but sets of interesting and engaging texts with several open-ended suggestions for teacher-tested high-quality strategy activities: a text about penguins might include a note-taking strategy; active vocabulary might revolve around a book about sharks. Suggestions and resources can be adapted to a particular circumstance while new ideas and modifications are added regularly. Teachers use this resource eagerly, emphasizing that it's more effective to advertise good instruction than to sell it. Imagine how quickly open-ended extension activities created by expert teachers multiply.

Choosing tier 2 instructional activities requires serious conversations and specific selection criteria. Tier 2 is not time to complete grade-level assignments, homework, or worksheets. Learning opportunities that failed to meet student needs at tier 1 will not suddenly become appropriate simply because students change from one setting to another. Tier 2 offers engaging, active learning in the context of real reading. This is what our tier 2 students need. This is what our tier 2 students deserve.

*L*earning opportunities that failed to meet student needs at tier 1 will not suddenly become appropriate simply because students change from one setting to another.

Ongoing Formal and Informal Assessment

RTI guidelines specify progress monitoring during tier 2 interventions so that no time is wasted on instructional strategies that are not working. This makes sense: we don't want to continue instruction that is not successful. Assessment lets us determine whether an intervention should be continued, adjusted, or changed. Recommendations for RTI data collection vary, but the most common suggestion is at least every two weeks. In Codie's case, data was collected weekly since teachers were concerned that tier 3 may be needed. These assessments were integrated into learning activities so that no instructional time was lost. This is not always the case with RTI progress monitoring.

In theory, monitoring progress increases accountability and ensures success. In practice, it can easily usurp instruction time and risk that informal forms of assessment will be abandoned. We need to ensure interventions are working, but today's tools for progress monitoring do not necessarily provide this guarantee. Schools must honestly consider if the data will reveal information about the learning process that warrants the time required to collect it and whether other more informative and less time-consuming forms of assessment will be lost in the shuffle. Valuable information can be gleaned by asking students to verbalize their thinking in the context of a strategy.

Tier 2 instruction is adjusted to students' needs, so data must reflect the focus: to monitor progress in word recognition you might ask a student to quickly read a list of words; to monitor fluency, you may ask the student to read a passage out loud. Many schools monitor progress using curriculum-based one-minute probes. This is a booming business, so carefully compare alternatives that are more closely aligned to the reading process.

If someone other than the classroom teacher provides the tier 2 interventions, both teachers should conduct assessment concurrently. The tier 2 teacher assesses the student in the context of those interventions while the tier 1 teacher conducts in-class assessments to ensure that learning transfers to the regular classroom. Each teacher can add valuable information to support instructional decisions. (On the other hand, a classroom teacher who is not effectively using assessment in tier 1 will be equally ineffective in tier 2.)

The higher the instructional tier, the more challenging RTI data collection becomes, since it occurs with greater frequency. This is a far more serious issue than some RTI supporters would like us to believe and should be an important research topic in the future. Opting for alternative, more informal, assessments to support instruction should also be a topic of focus. These issues are discussed in detail in Chapter 6.

Team Decision Making and Collaboration

A key feature of RTI is that decisions about the level of support, specific instructional interventions, and movement between tiers are made by a team of individuals (to include parents) who have direct information about the child. Team members are knowledgeable about effective literacy and the school curriculum and work hand in hand with the tier 2 interventionist and the classroom teacher (who are key members of the team). Decisions are not dictated by rigid guidelines. For example, each decision the team made in relation to Codie's literacy program was based on his specific instructional needs rather than any commercial advice or product. Meetings always focus on the quality of the child's instructional experience and professional decision making. There is simply no substitute for expert teaching.

There is simply no substitute for expert teaching.

Team decision making ensures that many expert viewpoints are brought to bear in solving problems. Team members vary from school to school but includes anyone with pertinent information, such as a school nurse (medical), counselor (social/emotional), or psychologist (diagnostic). The speech teacher was included in Codie's case due to his history of ear infections and difficulty with certain speech sounds. The team always includes the administrator, teachers providing instruction, and others in leadership roles (reading specialist, literacy coach, special education/Title 1 teacher)

The RTI team is a supportive collaboration. The role of the team is not to make decisions for interventionists, but to offer a springboard to think more deeply about each aspect of instruction. Good team members ask more questions than they answer. They emphasize how to adjust the intensity and specificity of interventions such as decreasing group size or duration and frequency of sessions. The team uses all available information to determine whether students should return to tier 1, continue tier 2, or move to tier 3. The interventionist and classroom teachers are central role to this process since they have an insider's viewpoint. If the interventionist is an expert teacher, this trust is warranted.

Team meetings are brief and focused, maintaining a comprehensive perspective by considering all available information. The goal is use this information to create an appropriate instructional plan (a road map with detours to allow for professional judgment). RTI literature emphasizes that the discussion is "data based," but ongoing informal assessments should also be considered. Meetings are not reduced to lamenting lack of parental support or the child's behavior; rather, they should lead to concrete solutions for helping struggling learners. A moderator and standard agenda will ensure that discussions are productive and positive at all times. This is a time to solve problems, not become mired in a counterproductive process.

If a team approach is not used, collaboration between tiers is even more critical. Effective tier 2 instruction must support tier 1 instruction, so both teachers (if there are two) need to share information that allows interventions to be as effective as possible. If the tier 2 teacher has success with a particular strategy, it makes sense to share this strategy with the classroom teacher so that it can be used in tier 1 as well. On the other hand, the classroom teacher may highlight a student's interest in a new topic or growing sight word knowledge.

Madeline's Story

To emphasize the four key features of tier 2 intervention, I'd like to introduce Madeline, a fourth-grade student. Madeline's struggle is a fairly recent development since she was previously a very successful reader. Within a few months after the new school year started, Madeline had gone from thriving to at-risk. She had difficulty answering the most explicit, in-the-book questions and could not remember key details. Her negative feelings about school were rapidly escalating to the point that she avoided any reading related activities.

The reading specialist scheduled an initial meeting with the parents and tier 1 teacher to determine what led to this change. The tier 1 teacher was an excellent reading teacher, but she was uncertain how to support Madeline. The tier 1 teacher shared that content area texts were a central part of the reading program including her small group instruction. The reading specialist felt that this was important information, knowing that other teachers used limited informational reading.

Suspecting that this new text structure was a factor, the reading specialist set out to gather information to support establishing instructional goals. He observed lessons in her classroom reading program and noted that Madeline seemed to possess few strategies to meet the new text demands. Strategies she used successfully with narrative texts were largely ineffective and technical vocabulary was challenging. She could not answer even basic content questions or recall key details. Her frustration was apparent.

Madeline's rapid downward spiral required immediate support, but the reading specialist was not convinced that tier 2 was an appropriate placement. He conducted running records using fourth-grade texts from the regular classroom. Madeline faltered every time she came to technical vocabulary and could not answer key questions or recall important details. He initiated a simple open-ended note-taking strategy and found that Madeline's understanding and recall increased. He modeled several vocabulary strategies; in particular demonstrating how to use text clues to determine the meaning of unfamiliar words. While Madeline still faltered, he could see a glimmer of progress even in this single session.

The reading specialist returned to the tier 1 teacher with these findings. He offered to demonstrate several instructional strategies in whole group and small group settings. After each model, time was provided for collaboration so that the tier 1 teacher could ask questions. Together they created some note-taking and vocabulary rituals that would support Madeline while she was learning study strategies for this new text structure. The reading specialist scheduled three thirty-minute sessions to jump-start this learning.

The tier 1 teacher found that these strategies were effective for all students, so she initiated them with the whole class. She incorporated vocabulary and study strategies into small group guided reading with informational texts. The teacher knew that Madeline wanted to be a veterinarian and loved animals so she used *National Geographic Explorer* collection of leveled readers as well as *Time for Kids* news magazines. Every student expressed enthusiasm for these additions so she added two new sections to her classroom library: news magazines and animal books. The tubs were almost always empty. She implemented "adopt a book bin" and placed Madeline in charge of the animal tub. A photograph of each student was placed on the front of the adopted bin. That child was the "'expert"' of the tub and was responsible to keep the selections organized.

The tier 1 teacher also initiated several strategies to differentiate instruction for her learners. She used a variety of jigsaw activities that allowed each student to become the expert of a specific text selection or topic. Students worked diligently in small groups to read information and record notes. They used these notes to teach peers their expert text and recorded concepts that peers taught them. Madeline quickly became known as the animal expert and was lovingly dubbed "Dr. Mattie" by her peers.

The reading specialist knew that Madeline's struggle could be addressed at tier 1 with a limited amount of support so entry into tier 2 was not needed. The tier 1 teacher simply needed a second pair of eyes and ears and time to collaborate with that person. Tier 2 played only a supportive role, although some schools might have labeled Madeline at risk and "committed" her to one program or another. Instead, she regained her rightful place as a successful reader while helping her teacher to become a better reading teacher.

The reading specialist conducted after-school sessions related to study strategies across all grades. Every teacher began to place more emphasis on informational texts, helping children navigate text features such as the index, glossary, captions, and graphs to understand text. These strategies impacted the success of every teacher. Tier 2 innovations became a conduit to expert teaching.

Answering the Hard Questions

Madeline's story reminds us that flexibility is a crucial element of the multi-tiered model. While the involvement of tier 2 was needed in her case, placement was not. Collaboration and professional support led to simple adjustments at tier 1 that had a domino effect on instruction across the board. An effective RTI framework explores changes that the tier 1 teacher can make instead of relegating the problem to tier 2. This flexibility requires each school to respond to challenging questions that will ensure an effective tier 2.

Who Should Provide Tier 2 Intervention?

Selecting a tier 2 interventionist is an important decision: it impacts both the quality of tier 2 instruction and the need for tier 3 intervention. The tier 2 interventionist may be the classroom teacher, school support staff such as the Title 1 teacher or reading specialist, or someone hired specifically for this purpose. It is essential that this person be qualified to provide instruction for students who are already lagging behind their peers. Some schools may need to redistribute resources to be responsive as needs change.

Many schools assign tier 2 interventions to the classroom teacher, but there are cautions to consider. Classroom teachers are responsible for general literacy instruction, differentiation, and interventions at tier 1; the added responsibility may cause frustration to the point that the quality of instruction at both tiers is compromised. Nor does it make sense to ask a teacher struggling to provide high-quality instruction at tier 1 to add tier 2 instruction; ineffective tier 1 instruction carried forward to tier 2 will only compound the problem and students will suffer the consequences.

Another disadvantage of assigning classroom teachers to tier 2 is that there is a risk that these interventions will substitute for those at tier 1. This defeats the purpose, since students will not get the *more* that they need; we are merely trading one setting for another. If the classroom teacher provides tier 2 interventions, this instruction must be added into the schedule. It may be best to use classroom teachers for tier 2 only after RTI has been in operation for at least a year to provide more time for ongoing professional development. This will ensure high-quality instruction at tier 2.

Ask these questions before deciding to use the classroom teacher for tier 2:

- Is additional time allotted beyond tier 1 instruction and interventions?
- Is tier 1 instruction effective and differentiated?
- Is the teacher highly qualified in the specific area of need?
- Are varied resources other than grade-level material readily accessible?
- Is ongoing professional development in place to support tier 2 interventions?
- Is there a means of professional collaboration and dialogue?

Some schools assign tier 2 intervention to instructional assistants, somehow justifying placing the most instructionally needy students with those who know the least about literacy. Failing to provide high-quality instruction at tier 2 is likely to result in more intensive support needs later. Some schools provide training for assistants, but it is rarely enough. At the very least, such a program requires intensive ongoing training and long-term mentoring, with an expert teacher in the wings at all times. In the end, an expert teacher is the most logical choice. If we cut corners in our attempt to equalize the instructional playing field, our students' learning gap will widen and we will be responsible.

When and How Often Should Tier 2 Intervention Be Provided?

RTI guidelines specify that students in tier 2 receive an additional thirty minutes of daily instruction *beyond tier 1.* This offers the support and the accelerated learning they need to begin to catch up with their peers. For tier 2 instruction to be *additional instruction*, it must be scheduled separately from tier 1 reading instruction and interventions. Classroom reading instruction must be protected from all interference, including tier 2 interventions.

C lassroom reading instruction must be protected from all interference, including tier 2 interventions.

Many schools accomplish this with an interdisciplinary plan, integrating literacy with science or social studies (math doesn't lend itself to this approach). The tier 2 teacher can then teach literacy across content areas while emphasizing these strategies in other contexts. This will require additional resources such as small sets of high-quality informational texts. Most publishing representatives can help the school find titles that reflect curriculum goals. *National Geographic* is an outstanding resource for this purpose.

An alternative is to conduct tier 2 interventions before or after school, as long as students do not view this as punitive. This is a good way to add more time to the ticking educational clock and most parents are likely to approve.

Some schools pay expert teachers a stipend to provide this instruction. This extra support needs to be presented to students as *engaging* enrichment. Children are exquisitely attuned to where they stand in relation to peers, and if they perceive these classes negatively, it will impede their success.

You can implement RTI gradually. Flexibility may be necessary in the beginning. For example, tier 2 interventions may initially be scheduled in twenty-minute sessions and increased to thirty minutes as schools work out the kinks. Twenty minutes daily is better than no minutes, and three days a week is better than no days. The reverse is also true: a group may receive forty minutes of daily instruction when this is warranted. Consistency is important in that twenty-minute daily sessions are preferable to forty-minute sessions twice weekly.

Where Should Tier 2 Intervention Be Provided?

When the tier 1 teacher is responsible for tier 2 intervention, instruction may occur in the classroom *provided it is separate from general reading instruction*. In this case, a specific time may be designated for tier 2 interventions by grade level. An instructional assistant or other support staff member rotates to classrooms to monitor students as they work on meaningful independent activities in other subjects such as social studies or science. This will free the teacher to work with tier 2 literacy groups in the classroom or in a separate location. A good approach is to substitute less important activities such as programmed instruction via a computer for tier 2 interventions. This requires no added support, results in no lost instruction, and is a better use of time.

When provided by someone other than the classroom teacher, tier 2 intervention may be either push-in or pull-out. In a push-in model, a support staff member such as the special education or Title 1 teacher or reading specialist can provide instruction in the classroom. In a pull-out approach, students are removed from the classroom. (Advantages and disadvantages of these approaches are discussed in Chapter 2.) Every option should be considered. If space permits, teachers providing intervention may have supplies on a cart so they can meet with small groups in areas close to the classroom. This minimizes travel time for students and offers opportunities to exchange information with the classroom teacher. Some schools form tier 2 groups comprised of students from several classrooms or even grade levels. This is a dangerous prospect, however, as it is easy for teachers to relinquish responsibility ("This is not my student"). This can also quickly turn into fixed-ability grouping. Unless groups are regularly adjusted and these teachers have the opportunity to collaborate, this approach is strongly discouraged.

How Long Should Tier 2 Intervention Last?

Most experts suggest that a tier 2 intervention can span eight to twelve weeks, or an average of from forty to sixty sessions. A general rule of thumb is that tier 2 interventions should not exceed eighteen weeks unless the reasons for doing so have been carefully considered. Tier 2 support is temporary; we do not want to continue it for too long without exploring other options such as adjusting tier 1 instruction or moving the student to tier 3. Neither, however, do we want to withhold support. Students may receive one or two rounds of tier 2 intervention. A second round is appropriate if students are making progress but simply need more time. In this case, you may want to decrease the size of the group or lengthen the sessions.

Flexibility in movement between tiers is also essential. Students may be returned to tier 1 full time, remain in tier 2 for a second round of instruction, or move to tier 3 for still more intense intervention. A student may move directly from tier 1 to tier 3 if careful consideration shows this to be in the child's best interests. Students may also move from tier 2 to tier 3 very quickly if it's apparent that the higher tier will be a more appropriate setting. RTI is about putting students first using flexible guidelines rather than hard-and-fast rules. It is important to weigh every option.

How Can We Increase Instructional Intensity?

GREEN

Tier 2 intervention increases the intensity of instruction. This is done initially by reducing the group size and increasing the duration and frequency of support in addition to the general literacy curriculum.

We can also intensify the type of instruction provided. Professional development should emphasize the following tactics to ensure high-quality instruction:

- Maintain high expectations but adjust support to accommodate each student.
- Use whole-to-part-to-whole teaching to ensure learning in meaningful contexts.
- Increase teacher think-alouds that make reading strategies explicit.
- Illustrate key points with specific oral and written examples.
- Check for understanding by soliciting responses beyond yes or no.
- Provide engaging feedback to reinforce understanding and address confusions.
- Coach students as they apply strategies in the course of reading.
- Scaffold support in the early stages while promoting independence.

- Reinforce new learning at spaced intervals.

- Redirect off-task behavior to avoid getting sidetracked.

- Offer individualized guidance to ensure understanding.

- Adjust the pace of instruction to student need.

- Encourage students to restate or paraphrase learning.

- Break learning into smaller increments and allow ample time to review key points.

- Make learning visible by using charts, graphs, illustrations, and diagrams.

- Use prompts or cues at first, gradually withdrawing them to promote independence.

- Engage students in conversations that revolve around learning.

- Highlight in-the-head strategies used by good readers.

- Monitor understanding at all times and reteach as needed.

- Summarize key concepts at the end of every lesson.

- Provide more time to practice new learning or apply learning in other contexts.

- Focus on only one or two skills at a time for deeper understanding.

- Give students ample wait time for reflection before expecting them to respond.

Designing Tier 2 Interventions

Once we determine that a student's needs are significant enough to warrant tier 2, we need to decide what that instruction will be. We cannot assume that instruction that did not work at tier 1 will work in a smaller setting. We need to take a different, more focused approach with coordination between tiers. But what should that approach be?

The source of instruction is the first point of disagreement. Too often I see educators insist it should be a scripted program, implemented without adapting it (which often translates to "with minimal thought"). I've emphasized that teachers are integral to RTI; this is especially true at higher tiers. If the time and energy used to promote scripts were spent on training reading teachers, I have no doubt we could make remarkable gains. Best of all, money saved on programs can be used to acquire differentiated resources chosen by these newly qualified teachers. Noddings (2008) makes the point thus: "If teachers want to teach students to think, they must think about what they themselves are doing" (12). We must resist any effort to reduce RTI to a superficial, controlling model or there may be no taking back the reins in the future.

*W*e must resist any effort to reduce RTI to a superficial, controlling model or there may be no taking back the reins in the future.

RED

Another controversy in the field concerns the instruction itself. Remarkably, many assert that tier 2 interventions focus on isolated skills, generally in *one* of the five pillars. This is not to say that isolation is not warranted, but that it cannot substitute for authentic contexts. Even if a program is used to "guide" instruction, it must engage students in real reading. According to Tooms et al. (2007), programs that "ask students to engage in activities that don't involve real reading should be avoided" (136). We need programs that are less "programlike" with a focus on meaningful reading that includes professional judgment.

We must distinguish between remediation and intervention to ensure a focus on the latter. Remediation typically is a pull-out approach with long-term support, while interventions accelerate learning to increase the possibility that the students will return to the classroom quickly. Remediation rarely coordinates with tier 1 and often replaces it, while interventions complement a general literacy program. Remediation often substitutes for effective reading instruction by focusing on reading games, skill and drill, or artlike activities, while interventions emphasize meaningful interactions with print. Remediation often uses grade-level material that necessitates excessive levels of support, while interventions match material to students.

The chart below provides an overview of these distinctions:

REMEDIATION	INTERVENTION
• Focus on "fixing" an existing problem	• Focus on preventing or stopping failure
• Instruction that is "instead of"	• Instruction that is "in addition to"
• Replaces classroom reading instruction	• Enhances classroom reading instruction
• Little if any adjustment in intensity	• Adjusts the intensity of instruction
• Targets a single isolated skill	• Focuses on the reading process
• Pull-out program	• Approach varies according to need
• Material that is either too easy or too hard	• Material that reflects a gradient of difficulty
• Slow-paced instruction that simply waters down the curriculum	• Fast-paced instruction to promote acceleration
• Often fails to achieve mastery	• Repeated practice to achieve mastery
• Emphasis on long-term support	• Emphasis on short-term support
• Separation from general education	• Coordination with the general education program
• Limited ongoing assessment	• Emphasis on ongoing assessment

Only thirty minutes daily is allotted for tier 2 instruction, so every minute has to count. If most of this time is spent on isolated skills, we miss the point of good reading instruction. RTI is our chance to rethink what instruction for struggling readers—or good instruction in general—should look like, sound like, and feel like. Students need to read, not pretend to read or get ready to read or talk about getting ready to read. The majority of time is spent reading and discussing texts to build strategic knowledge and thoughtful reading. Tier 2 instruction integrates key literacy components in the context of reading.

The texts students read are equally important. Struggling readers need a wide range of texts they can read and understand (Allington 2006a)—interesting texts (many of them informational) they *want* to read. Their experiences with these texts must include teacher modeling in the form of think alouds, as well as direct instruction in how to use reading strategies with information text structures (Duke 2000, 2004). Interesting expository texts are available at all levels. Of course, tier 2 instruction cannot be the only time in the day students read appealing texts at appropriate levels. Classroom teachers must also use these rich resources.

GREEN

To ensure the precious thirty minutes daily tier 2 time is used wisely, I'm going to make a radical suggestion: we need to clearly state the things that must *not* be part of this instruction—worksheets (including computerized versions), art activities (unless they are very brief and directly related to reading or visual literacy), "reading games" that are heavy on the game aspect and light on reading, and anything else that reduces reading to "stuff." No copying definitions from the dictionary. No fill-in-the-blanks. Students will not write words twenty times each. For teachers to understand what good instruction *is*, they must also understand what it *is not*.

Once we established what *not* to do, the "pie theory" will help us to identify what *to do*. Imagine a pie sitting on the table. The pie represents thirty minutes allotted for tier 2 instruction. It's the only pie we have, so we better divide it carefully. Begin by cutting it into two fifteen-minute halves. The first half of the pie represents the new book selected just for these students to promote independence and problem solving with the teacher's support. Reading this carefully chosen text reinforces what students know and engages them in using strategies in a meaningful context. The second half of the pie is subdivided into three five-minute sections for three key learning events: rereading familiar text, working with words, and integrating reading and writing. Students spend five minutes reading books they have previously read in intervention sessions. (This is a good time to take a running record or make anecdotal notes.) Word work may include any learning activity that reinforces sounds, words, and letters. The final five minutes can be used to integrate reading and writing, perhaps by writing a sentence about the story.

My pie plan is not as lockstep as it sounds (feel free to devote the entire session to reading the new text), but it makes clear that the bulk of tier 2 interventions should focus on real reading and writing activities. Brief isolated work on words, sounds, and concepts is included but doesn't overshadow reading. (Remember, anything addressed in isolation can also be addressed in the context of reading or writing.)

Intervention focuses on real books that are interesting, colorful, and engaging. Each child reads on her or his own as the teacher supports these efforts. Time isn't wasted waiting for peers to take turns during round-robin reading. Teachers do not dole out five questions to answer after reading but engage students in discussing texts at much deeper levels of understanding. Students are encouraged to generate and respond to their own questions. Conversations revolve around real books and the teacher can model key strategies in context.

As you plan with colleagues, build from this simple premise: *successful interventions engage students in meaningful reading and writing activities using interesting texts and tasks that guarantee a high level of success while integrating discrete reading skills in context.* Programs must maintain this focus.

Of course, teaching must be informed by student behavior. Tier 2 intervention is not initiated until teachers have had ample time to observe students in varied learning experiences. I liken it to the "roaming in the known" phase of Reading Recovery (Clay 1985): the first two weeks are devoted to informal assessment of students engaged in learning to help teachers discover their strengths, needs, and interests. Instruction is initiated only after we have a clearer understanding that will support their instructional decisions. Knowledge becomes power and enhances instruction at every tier. This is far more valuable than looking at charts that relegate learners to mere numbers. Of course, collaboration with other teachers will provide a double dose of "roaming" information.

It's hard to describe precisely what high-quality tier 2 instruction looks like, but you can recognize it in an instant. Effective tier 2 teachers focus on meaningful contexts to reinforce and extend learning. Effective tier 2 teachers use resources but rely heavily on their own professional responsibility. These teachers trust their instincts and have the confidence and knowledge to ask good questions as they arise. They insist on high-success learning experiences using interesting, engaging, and motivating texts that match student need at all times. In short, effective tier 2 teachers view their students as living, breathing instructional informants.

Maintaining Flexibility of Purpose

Teachers often ask me if thirty minutes is enough time for interventions. My response is always the same: "Yes, *if* what we choose to do with that thirty minutes is of the highest quality and targeted to students' needs." Good teaching is not about the time allotted but how we choose to spend that allotted time. It's depth over breadth. Some teachers think learning can't occur if the book isn't thick enough or there aren't enough skills. Effective teachers opt for deeper levels of engagement rather than a surface knowledge of concepts.

Tier 2 intervention is based on the idea that *less leads to more*, a message in direct conflict with the current focus on teaching to the test and a bulging curriculum. We know that instruction is more powerful when we limit teaching points to one or two or focus on key ideas. Students have time to revisit and review learning when text selections are brief and emphasize limited concepts. We promote long-term knowledge over short-term memorization that quickly fades. Feedback and guidance are embedded in instruction and time to practice new learning is nonnegotiable. Tier 2 teachers can achieve miraculous things in the allotted time because they use every minute with this goal clearly in view.

Flexibility is also emphasized at tier 2. For some students, tier 2 intervention occurs at the start of the year. For example, if a student was placed in tier 2 toward the end of the previous year, tier 2 instruction may be initiated immediately the following year, before schoolwide screening is completed. It's not the child's fault the year ran out. If our decisions are based on our students' needs, exceptions are always possible. Guidelines *guide* decision making but don't take precedence over students—not if we truly care about making RTI everything it promises to be.

This flexible view should be applied to tier 2 programs and lesson plans as well. Some experts emphasize that tier 2 teachers should "consistently follow a lesson plan." However, a multi-angle view of RTI accommodates using lesson plans as a guide that can be adjusted as necessary. In thirty-seven years, I have never seen a lesson plan that can anticipate the needs of students as they are actively engaged in learning. Learning is messy business, and there's no way to anticipate what students may say or how they will respond. It takes a knowledgeable professional to respond intentionally to these often surprising events. Tier 2 teachers are the most highly qualified reading teachers, so their instincts should count at least as much a prescribed lesson plan. After all, a lesson plan without knowledge of students is little more than an outsider's guesswork. Be selective and assume a broader view.

The question about selecting interventions is both critical and challenging. There are many outstanding intervention programs available such as Reading

Recovery and Fountas and Pinnell Leveled Literacy (LLI) (http://www.fountas andpinnellleveledliteracyintervention.com/)—and there are others that are highly suspect. Answering several important questions will reinforce key points in this chapter and help us discriminate between effective and ineffective intervention programs and resources (these questions also will apply at tier 3):

- Is tier 2 support in addition to the support offered at tier 1?
- Are instructional efforts coordinated between tiers 1 and 2?
- Is the instructional framework rich and flexible enough to be used at any tier?
- Is instruction based on highly engaging activities and teacher-student interactions?
- Is the most appropriate instructional setting considered for that child and reviewed regularly?
- Does instruction teach skills while emphasizing application of skills in real texts?
- Are high-quality text resources at gradually challenging levels offered to support the instructional recommendations?
- Does the group size remain small with an emphasis on groups of three?
- Is the focus on accelerated progress over remediation?
- Are the same instructional strategies reinforced at tier 1 for repeated practice and transfer?
- Is there a home–school connection with appropriate resources?
- Is there an emphasis on professional development so that expert teachers are providing the instruction?
- Does the program include a rich assessment piece that incorporates both summative and formative data?

We must take great care to offer the most effective instruction possible at tier 2, but we cannot view tier 2 as high-quality instruction afforded only some. We must ensure that every child has access to the same level of excellence, regardless of the source of that instruction. The RTI framework embraces tiers equally in design and implementation as one-tier supports, builds on, and enriches the next. A multi-sided view emphasizes quality instruction within *and* beyond tier 2. How could we possibly opt for anything less?

It seems only fitting to return to Nikolai's three questions: *When is the best time to do things? Who is the most important one? What is the right thing to do?* Our answers to each of these questions can guide our efforts to maintain a student-centered view of tier 2. These are the questions expert teachers ask on a day-to-day and student-to-student basis and the answers will help us to maintain our sights on what is most important in our instructional world.

CHAPTER 5

Tier 3 Intervention: Intensifying the Instructional Support

I have great faith in a seed. Convince me that you have a seed there, and I am prepared to expect wonders.

—Henry David Thoreau

Some people are naturals at acquiring computer know-how. They make life in the technological fast lane seem like easy street. I am not one of those people. When technology beyond a simple cell phone became mandatory in my personal and professional life, I gave it the old college try to get up to speed, but those computer manuals may as well be written in a foreign language. It soon became clear that I needed a helping hand.

Enter Alex and Todd. One or both of these brilliant young men come to my home to tackle my latest conundrum. We sit side by side in front of my computer. They model the strategy first and then let me try it as they wait in the wings, ready to offer a nudge when I falter. They don't tell—they suggest. They ask questions to guide my understanding, keeping me engaged in the process at all times. They never push me out of my comfort zone; I get undivided attention in a nonthreatening environment. They assess of the look of confusion on my face and continue to model in a new direction until the cloud lifts. My coaches have stimulated a hitherto dormant part of my brain. This strange new world is slowly becoming a little less strange.

Alex and Todd's instructional style is an apt model for the kind of interaction that needs to occur in tier 3 RTI intervention. They represent every aspect of the high level of support needed in the third line of defense for getting struggling readers back on track. Tier 3 intervention offers intensive, individualized support targeted to the specific needs of faltering readers. It immerses learners in an active process within meaningful contexts. It focuses heavily on the gradual release of responsibility using demonstrations and modeling, shared and guided practice, and independent application. This individualized instructional support is invaluable when students learn a new skill (Taberski 2000): "We need the 'expert' to watch what we're doing, and then show us a better way" (125). Our literacy learners need the same dependable expert advice I get from Alex and Todd. This can come only from an expert reading teacher.

Distinguishing Between Tier 2 and Tier 3

I could save a great deal of time by making this chapter one short sentence: "Ditto to everything in Chapter 4, times two." Every point that was made relative to tier 2 is equally important at tier 3, in higher doses. Tier 3 increases instructional intensity further by decreasing the size of the group to one-on-one or up to three students and increasing the frequency and duration to two thirty-minute daily sessions. These adjustments are critical for students who need more help than tier 2 can offer.

The following chart provides an overview of the distinctions between tier 2 and tier 3. Tier 3 students are likely to have more significant learning needs than those at tier 2, but the instructional strategies look much the same.

TIER	PERCENT OF STUDENTS	FREQUENCY OF INTERVENTION	INSTRUCTIONAL GROUP SIZE	DATA COLLECTION	INSTRUCTIONAL INTERVENTIONIST
Tier 2	10–15 percent	One 30-minute daily session	3–5 students (3 preferable)	Every two weeks	Classroom teacher or other
Tier 3	5–10 percent	Two 30-minute daily sessions	1–3 students (1 preferable)	Weekly	Expert reading teacher

Tier 3 intervention is generally referred to as *strategic* or *intensive*. As the top rung in an RTI ladder, tier 3 offers the highest level of instructional intensity. Hall (2008) says, "The instruction is characterized by extraordinary intensity and focus" (68–69). The word e*xtraordinary* is an apt descriptor, because it highlights the heightened instruction needed for students who do not respond to the combined support of tiers 1 and 2. As the last line of defense before options such as special education are considered, tier 3 literacy instruction has to be potent and effective.

Tier 3 support is *in addition to* a classroom literacy program, so sessions are not scheduled during the regular literacy lesson or workshop. It is preferable to schedule two thirty-minute daily sessions rather than a single sixty-minute session to break learning into smaller segments and reinforce new learning. This requires creative scheduling with an integrated approach to literacy. Tier 3 instruction can be offered in conjunction with science and social studies lessons, as long as the reading material is appropriate.

Selecting the Instructional Interventionist for Tier 3

Much of the RTI literature states that the tier 3 interventionist can be a classroom teacher or someone designated by the school. However, it says nothing about the qualifications of this person. Tier 3 is far too critical a stage for such an open-ended, namby-pamby guideline. The idea that classroom teachers will become tier 3 interventionists worries me since it will likely overburden teachers already responsible for the general literacy curriculum, differentiated instruction, and tier 1 intervention (and perhaps tier 2 interventions). Tier 3 is demanding and time-consuming, so quality instruction at all tiers will likely be jeopardized. Worse, if a classroom teacher is struggling to offer high-quality instruction at tier 1, placing that teacher at tier 3 will mean that these students receive two doses of poor instruction.

Students in tier 3 have the most severe reading problems, so we must ensure that the interventionist is an expert reading teacher. We must also ensure that the general education students receive is of the highest quality so that the support students receive at both tier 1 and tier 3 works in concert. When the interventionist is not the same person at tier 1 and tier 3, the classroom teacher gains a second set of eyes and ears. Each teacher has a unique perspective that can support instruction as long as collaboration is built into the day.

Many schools use Title 1 or special education teachers or reading specialists for tier 3 instruction. The designation of "expert" reading teacher still applies—

a title is not necessarily accompanied by requisite qualifications. Reading specialists with minimal training (and astoundingly, they're out there) are not the best choice for tier 3 instruction. Some schools hire expert teachers specifically for this purpose while others pay a stipend to expert teachers on their staff to conduct all or some tier 3 instruction before or after the school day. These are all options if the candidate is a highly qualified reading teacher.

Assuming the tier 3 interventionist is someone other than the classroom teacher, instruction usually occurs in a pull-out setting. Designate a specific area such as a small room with a table large enough for three students to work with a teacher. Some question my emphasis on a pull-out approach, which inevitably leads to time lost in transit. But if we offer high-quality, accelerated, *temporary* support with the intent to return students to the classroom program as soon as possible, this configuration can work well.

We can maximize this approach by offering the classroom teacher professional support and collaboration to coordinate efforts. In this way, Tier 3 can be a springboard to high-quality tier 1 classroom instruction. Tier 3 teachers can model an instructional strategy to extend interventions across tiers. This may occur by giving classroom teachers time to observe lessons or the interventionist may model a procedure in the classroom. This will enhance classroom instruction, ensure coordination between tiers, and engage teachers in ongoing professional collaboration.

Progress monitoring occurs with greater frequency at tier 3, generally cited as weekly or daily. Making certain that we are not wasting time for students who do not have time to waste on instruction that isn't working is a worthy goal. But this attempt not to waste time may do just that! Assessment inevitably usurps some instructional time regardless of how quick the measurement. The assumption that increased assessment leads to increased quality of instruction is not necessarily the case. Assessment can come from many sources that are less time-consuming and more informative. This is discussed in detail in Chapter 6.

The Relationship Between Special Education and Tier 3

The relationship between tier 3 intervention and special education is a prevailing disagreement. Some view tier 3 synonymous with special education in that entry into tier 3 is entry into special education. Others view tier 3 as one more tier of support separate from special education, a precursor that may or may not lead to referral. In practice, most schools consider tier 3 separate from special education or add a fourth or fifth tier to allow more leeway before a special education label is applied.

I contend that this latter approach is preferable, for two reasons. First, if tier 3 is special education, students get "labeled" before they can be caught by this safety net. Second, while the top tier of an RTI model offers concentrated support in very small settings, special education sometimes brings a *decrease* in instructional intensity. Special education teachers often serve many students, so groups are much larger than they would be during tier 3 intervention. It isn't logical to opt for a support system that eliminates the intensity otherwise available at tier 3.

To further complicate the problem, special education is often separate from and uncorrelated with general education and an open line of communication with classroom teachers is rare. Tier 3 provides a short-term support offered until students can get back on track. This has not historically been the case with special education where many students are caught in a web from which they cannot escape. Entry into tier 3 is also faster than entry into special education. A broader view of tier 3 also allows students to enter (or reenter) tier 3 after they exit special education to help to alleviate the regression often seen after these services cease. Students can also receive support as special education referral and testing take place. This makes good sense.

The argument that this approach withholds special education services for too long does not stand up if the intended flexible nature of tiers is honored. The recommended schedule of support at tier 3 is the same as tier 2: eight to ten weeks or not to exceed eighteen. But movement between any tier does not occur according to rigid guidelines and it is not necessarily a linear movement. Students move up or down between tiers according to their needs and when they need it. If those needs are clearly greater than can be addressed within the tiers, referral to special education can be initiated as early as tier 1. In some cases, tier 3 is sufficient to successfully return students to a general education setting. In other cases, failure to respond warrants special education referral. If a child qualifies, tier 3 offers a short-term safety net until formal placement. Otherwise, tier 3 continues. In this case, tier 3 increases the support options we make available.

Julian's Story

To understand the flexible nature of a tier 3 that puts students at the center, let's look at Julian. Julian, a sixth grade student, entered this RTI school at the beginning of the year. Initial screening reflected that her reading level was mid grade 2. Not surprisingly, Julian showed many signs of frustration and worked hard to avoid reading-related activities. She clearly would not be successful with the grade-level curriculum, even with modification and differentiation. This was confirmed by the initial screening and informal assessment.

A Title 1 teacher responsible for tier 3 interventions reviewed information and met with the classroom teacher. Parent records showed that Julian's struggle began after suffering a bike accident in second grade that initiated a gradual spiral in school. They described normal school achievement before the accident, but progress stopped almost immediately. Her previous school did not recommend assessment and she was released from medical care for reasons that were unknown by the parents. The classroom teacher shared that Julian had difficulty concentrating and remembering information, even when it was presented orally. This was consistent with the information provided by parents.

A team meeting was called with the principal, Title 1 teacher, classroom teacher, school diagnostician, and special education teacher. Unfortunately, her previous school did not offer the RTI safety net currently available. They discussed the dramatic gap in Julian's performance, voicing concern that there could be a learning disability brought on by the injury. The team agreed that a special education referral was warranted. In the interim, Julian was placed directly in tier 3 since tier 2 was not intensive enough. The Title 1 teacher, an expert reading teacher, modeled several memory techniques in the general education setting such as frequent review, mind mapping, and tape-recorded lessons.

When special education testing was completed, it was determined that Julian qualified and she exited tier 3 for placement in special education. Notice that Julian did not have to bide her time waiting for referral and testing, but was able to access the tiered framework for the support she needed right away. In addition, the tier 1 teacher was given strategies to support Julian in the regular classroom. Certainly, reading will likely be a long-term struggle in Julian's case—but every measure was taken to ensure her success. She began to make many gains and became a happier and more engaged learner.

GREEN

Designing Tier 3 Interventions

The instructional strategies used in tier 2 intervention—modeling and demonstrating, coaching and prompting, reinforcing existing knowledge, providing ongoing feedback, encouraging active engagement, dividing learning into smaller segments, reviewing and repeating information in many contexts—are also used at tier 3, with more intensity. (See the key instructional goals discussed on pages 60–61.)

Scaffolding is a term first used by Wood, Bruner, and Ross (1976) to describe the support teachers offer students so children can successfully participate in learning experiences they would not otherwise be able to. Scaffolding allows teachers to work within the child's *zone of proximal development* (Vygotsky 1978). When teachers offer just the right amount of scaffolding, they can encourage problem solving and strategy use; they then gradually withdraw this support as students become more independent. In this way, students learn self-correcting strategies that increase their comprehension. As students participate in these important learning experiences over time, they develop what Clay referred to as a "self-extending system" (1985). This places instructional emphasis on teaching children the strategies that will help them to become more independent in the future—in and beyond any instructional setting. This independence is always key.

Wong, Groth, and O'Flahavan (1994) explored the teacher's role in scaffolding by examining teacher-student interactions in Reading Recovery lessons. Researchers recorded teachers' comments during each lesson in an effort to determine what teachers did to scaffold learning and support students in the context of reading. They found that teachers used five types of scaffolding comments: telling, modeling, prompting, coaching, and discussing. They provided more support when a new text was introduced than when students read a familiar text.

During these teacher-student interactions, the teachers viewed reading from the students' perspective. By attempting to understand students' thinking, they were able to better promote "in-the-head" strategies and help students pay attention to meaning. Through scaffolding, they made students an active part of the reading process, taught new strategies, and encouraged independent problem solving.

An important finding of the research is that expert teachers do more coaching than telling (this is supported by Taylor et al. 2002). The opposite is also true; inexperienced teachers do more telling than modeling, prompting, coaching, and discussing. Telling students a word or explaining its meaning provides more scaffolding than students need and does little to make them active problem solvers or increase their independence. Telling is not teaching.

The intense support needed by tier 3 students means that every minute must be spent wisely. Again, we begin by stating activities that will *not* take place during tier 3 instruction—worksheets or fill-in-the blank activities (on paper or the computer). Tier 3 intervention is not the time to complete an art project or play games. It is time devoted to rich instructional and reinforcement activities.

Unfortunately, computer-centered activities are central components of many commercial programs that are recommended for tier 3 intervention, on the grounds that "less teacher time is needed." This is an alarming statement: these students need more teacher interaction, not less. The idea that computerized instruction can compare with thoughtful modeling, coaching, prompting, and discussing is ludicrous. It suggests that we place far too much faith in "stuff" and far too little in the role of expert teachers.

Certainly some schools do not have access to the same professional resources in terms of expert reading teachers such as a reading specialist or coach. There is no question that computer software would be a less expensive alternative than hiring additional staff. Yet, we can better address these limitations by providing the professional development that will allow us to utilize the staff resources that are available. While it can be argued that computer-centered activities provide a better option than nothing—I would argue that the money spent on these passive resources would be far better invested in helping every teacher become more expert reading teachers. Well-designed staff development throughout the year is no more expensive than these passive and often expensive investments.

As in tier 2 intervention, the bulk of time is spent in authentic reading contexts with real texts focused on active engagement and teacher scaffolding. The "pie model" I introduced in Chapter 4 applies equally to tier 3—the only difference is that you now have two pies. Limiting the time for isolated skills does not mean that you are neglecting these critical features of reading; they're simply embedded in authentic reading experiences. This again makes meaningful, high-quality texts matched to the reading level of students the focus of instruction for tier 3. (These texts may also be used at other tiers; they are therefore best housed in a central location.) Such worthy small-group sets should include informational texts, even in the early grades (Duke 2000).

Some schools purchase a distinct program for tier 3 while others use the tier 2 program but ratchet up delivery. I have the same concern about both approaches, as I expressed for tier 2. First, a distinct program further disconnects each tier, particularly for students who move from tier 2 to tier 3. Second, expert teachers who provide tier 3 instruction warrant the freedom to use and modify resources in carefully designed approaches both in and beyond those programs. Yet this kind of flexibility is often "outlawed," requiring teachers to proceed precisely as specified. In some cases, this occurs when teachers fall under the spell of the program and feel that they cannot teach effectively if they deviate in any way (when the opposite is far more true). In other cases, school systems purchase these products and monitor whether teachers use them according to the step-by-step and page-by-page directive of the teacher's guide. In either case, good teaching is compromised by downplaying the role of teacher's professional judgment.

Valencia and Buly (2005) have demonstrated why relying on a single pack-aged resource is particularly ineffective at tier 3. They explored fourth graders who did not pass the state-mandated literacy test. In a group of students with the same numerical score, they found six unique clusters with different instruc-tional needs. Automatic word callers decoded words quickly and accurately but did not read for meaning. Struggling word callers were unable to read for mean-ing because they couldn't *identify* words. Word stumblers faltered at words but had good comprehension. The remaining clusters were slow comprehenders, slow word callers, and disabled readers. Clearly, instructional needs in each cluster varied.

This research should inform our instruction nationwide. It supports the premise that flexible and varied instruction—teacher modeling, shared and guided practice, and independent application—allows us to address student's individual needs. This research also underscores the wisdom of using a wide range of materials and resources that go far beyond those provided by pro-grams. Releasing a death grip on programs is essential, particularly at tier 3 when stakes are so high.

*R*eleasing a death grip on programs is essential, particularly at tier 3 when stakes are so high.

Kendall's Story

Let's turn to Kendall to illustrate an intervention design at tier 3. Kendall, a third grade student, had always attended this school. A successful kindergarten year prepared her for first grade, but she soon struggled. Her first grade teacher did not express concern until she recommended retention at the end of the year. Her parents refused and Kendall entered second grade. Her struggle escalated but her parents refused retention again. Kendall's first and second grade teacher did not differentiate, basing their literacy program on isolated phonics, whole-group instruction, and mountains of skill sheets—a marked departure from kindergarten where Kendall was immersed in authentic literacy.

The school initiated RTI at the beginning of Kendall's entry to third grade. The universal screening at this time showed that Kendall was reading at an early first grade level. Assessment reflected that she struggled to read with fluency and understanding—not surprising considering the gap between grade level and performance. The grade-level oral reading fluency screening scores were insufficient to support the team in identifying any specific instructional goals since Kendall could not read the selected texts.

The reading specialist reviewed Kendall's school records. Kendall's third grade teacher was known to be an excellent reading teacher who went to great lengths to ensure success for all students. She used a literature-based approach as the foundation of her literacy program. The basal reading program was used as a resource, but she insisted on matching books to students in varied settings. She taught skills and strategies with a variety of quality texts and viewed read-aloud, shared reading, and guided reading as key features of her day. She had a rich classroom library reflecting a wide reading range and carved out daily time in her schedule for enthusiastic, independent, self-selected reading.

The reading specialist began by scheduling time to observe Kendall in her third grade classroom. Kendall's struggle was apparent, although she seemed to have learned many strategies to compensate and readily put these things to use. She did not hesitate to select books from the classroom library, gravitating to easy texts. Her parents frequented the local library, so her enthusiasm was not surprising. She preferred humorous books, particularly those about animals. She did not appear frustrated, but it was clear that this was due to the tier 1 classroom design and support she received at home. Kendall rarely volunteered and avoided reading orally. She seemed to engage in literacy activities from a distance but rarely chose to actively participate.

The reading specialist conducted informal assessment. Kendall knew sixty-seven sight words from the district list of the first one hundred high-frequency words. This was fairly surprising given the results of an oral reading sample, since her knowledge didn't transfer to connected print. A running record was conducted and reflected a heavy reliance on letter-by-letter decoding. Kendall rarely used common patterns and labored with each word, even those she knew by sight. After laborious sounding out, she continued reading or made up a word with the initial letter, whether it made sense or not (*house/happy*). Her reading was halting and word-by-word, even with first grade material. When asked what strategy she used to figure out words she didn't know, she responded with a blank stare.

This assessment confirmed that Kendall was building a sight vocabulary but did not use known words in reading. Comprehension and fluency were low even with first grade material and she possessed few independent problem-solving behaviors. Kendall rarely reread or self-corrected words, appealed to the teacher often, and generally relied on decoding words over checking the meaning of the words she read. It was clear that Kendall's struggle would escalate as the year progressed.

A team meeting was scheduled to share all available information. The team decided that the classroom teacher would increase Kendall's guided reading to four days weekly and decrease the size of her group to three. With the help of the reading specialist, they gathered text resources from the schoolwide bookroom, emphasizing informational texts about animals and funny animal stories. Kendall was placed in tier 2 with a group of three students for a brief period to see how she responded. Both teachers established a common goal: high-utility reading patterns, cross-checking visual information with meaning, and promoting active in-the-head early strategies using modeling, coaching, and prompting in guided reading. They selected several brief word work activities to open and close the guided reading lesson and the same goals were emphasized in context.

At the end of three weeks, the teachers repeated the oral reading assessment and sight vocabulary list and determined that Kendall was making slow progress. The team then decided to place her in tier 3 to increase instructional intensity. This intensity provided the support she needed to begin to make steady gains. Kendall made dramatic progress with the added time and coordination of goals in the regular classroom.

After six weeks, the team decided that Kendall no longer needed the intensity of tier 3, but continued to need support. She reentered tier 2 for another six weeks in a group of five students. She made so much progress that she returned to the full support of tier 1. The reading specialist and tier 1 teacher continued to monitor her progress for several weeks. She made rapid gains and the gap between Kendall and her peers virtually closed by the end of the school year.

Kendall's success again underscores how crucial it is to keep movement between tiers fluid. She entered tier 2 immediately and did not have to play a waiting game for tier 3 when she did not make expected progress. Eventually, she returned to tier 2 and then back to the classroom where she made remarkable gains the rest of the year. This "ideal" RTI is unfettered by rigid schedules. The team found the time and data that was needed to ensure that Kendall did not have a learning disability. In Kendall's case, she suffered from an equally debilitating disability—a "teaching disability" that occurred in first and second grade. Students learn what we teach and Kendall had quite effectively learned to read in a letter-by-letter drill that was devoid of meaning. We cannot penalize our students for our failure to provide adequate instruction.

Kendall's struggle was a success story because her tier 1 teacher was willing to do whatever was needed to ensure her success. Instructional coordination in a flexible model accomplished this goal.

GREEN

Enriching Tier 3 Intervention Through Flexible Decisions

Tier 3 intervention provides the most concentrated instruction in the RTI framework. As noted earlier, this support is provided by decreasing the group size to one, two, or three and increasing the frequency and duration of instruction—five more hours of instruction every week, provided in two daily thirty-minute sessions. This intense instruction helps to distinguish between students who have a learning problem, or struggling readers, and those with a disability who need special education support. Tier 3 intervention is demanding and costly and requires additional resources, so schools must weigh every option carefully before initiating it.

An expert teacher should be seen as a nonnegotiable requirement of tier 3. This may be accomplished by using the available staff resources or providing adequate staff development that will help the school gain access to more expert teachers. Because the learning needs of these students spill over into the rest of the school day, collaboration is a key ingredient of success. The classroom teacher must be competent to support tier 3 instruction, and tier 3 interventionists can share important information that can be used in tier 1. If a classroom teacher cannot contribute in this way, professional development is needed. Combined effort of all tiers ensures good decisions across tiers.

For example, if a student completes one round of tier 2 intervention with only partial success, should he or she be placed in tier 3 or receive a second round of tier 2 in a smaller group? Always ask, "What is the most appropriate setting for *this* child in order to offer the level of support needed at this time?" Tier 3 is always an option if and when appropriate, but alternatives should be considered. Adjustments may be needed within tier 3: changing from small group to one-on-one instruction, adding ten minutes to a thirty-minute session, changing from pull-out to push-in. Continuous assessment leads to these adjustments and increases the success *for that child*. If we are not responsive to student needs, RTI can become ability grouping in a lockstep approach.

*I*f we are not responsive to student needs, RTI can become ability grouping in a lockstep approach.

Maintaining Flexibility of Purpose

An effective tiered RTI model is pliable enough for each tier to work in concert. It also helps teachers to distinguish a learning disability from a learning difference—or even a "school-induced" struggle. The goal of a tiered approach is not to eliminate special education: there will always be students who legitimately need this service. Rather, the goal is to use a wide range of support options so that learning disabilities are not misidentified. Even more important, the goal is to increase the quality of the general education instruction so that fewer students need RTI support in the first place. Every learning experience can inform the support options within or beyond an intervention. RTI doesn't close doors, it opens them.

The interaction between tiers is critical. Tier 3 instruction is only as effective as instruction offered at tier 2, which is only as effective as instruction offered at tier 1. Failure to ensure high-quality tier 1 instruction leads to too many tier 2 interventions that then lead to too many tier 3 interventions. RTI is effective only when instruction at every tier meets the same high standards. Cautiously and carefully providing a flexible menu of support options will richly benefits students *and* teachers and increase their potential for continued success in a positive learning environment for all.

Alex and Todd provide modeling, coaching, support, and feedback that have led to my growing confidence and competence with computers. Tier 3 offers the same support to students. We sit side by side, model the strategy and let them try it as we wait in the wings to offer a gentle nudge if they falter. We don't tell—we suggest. We ask questions that engage them in the process at all times. We provide undivided attention in a safe environment. We assess their confusion and offer a new direction until the cloud lifts. These supports are not packaged, but delivered by expert teachers who make responsible choices to meet the unique needs of students. In short, we bring sense to what must seem like a strange and complicated world. Our students deserve nothing less.

CHAPTER 6

Broadening the Role of Assessment in an RTI Model

*T*he best fertilizer is the gardener's shadow.

—Author unknown

My favorite new high-tech toy is my GPS, or global positioning system. This amazing tool fits in my suitcase and is quickly placed on the front window of any rental car. I type in the address of my final destination, push a button, and my new best friend magically identifies my location and translates directions graphically onto the screen. If I take a wrong turn, she kindly utters, "Recalculating" and sends new directions leading back to the right path. She knows where I've been, where I am, and where I'm going. She continuously monitors my status and offers a nudge if I stray.

Effective assessment works much like my GPS. It's *ongoing, embedded,* and *varied*—a tracking system to reflect where our students are at any given time. Each assessment offers a new entry to help us navigate toward academic success. Of course, a GPS is powerless without a knowledgeable user and a destination. In the same way, knowledgeable teachers have specific goals in mind and input new assessment information to recalculate the most logical path to a final destination.

But the comparison ends here, my friends. The cycle of assessment and instruction is about teachers and students, not microchips and data entry. As the knowledgeable user, *you* continuously input and respond to new data to make critical decisions that set the stage for the success or failure of your students. The challenge is to consider how this giant piece of the RTI puzzle fits into your daily teaching so that assessment does not become a GPS of forced destinations without side trips, detours, or time to stop to smell the roses. *You* are the missing piece because you possess the knowledge that weaves assessment and instruction. RTI must reposition the role of real teachers making critical instructional decisions based on ongoing and authentic assessment measures.

With this in mind, it is not my intent to recommend assessment tools or detail step-by-step procedures; this has been done extensively in other resources. My goal is to provide a lens to view assessment in an RTI model from a new perspective. The assessment component of RTI runs the greatest risk of falling on the "dark side," as emphasized by Farstrup (2008), "We must not allow narrowly defined screening tests to constrain or limit instruction provided under RTI. More than ever, teaching to tests that are cheaply administered but narrowly defined is neither appropriate nor productive" (21).

Exploring a New Framework for Effective Literacy Assessment

The changing role of assessment has escalated to new heights in the United States since the 2001 NRP report, as instruction has been slowly forced into a secondary role. Today's high-stakes tests that focus on accountability are frequently designed to measure achievement for teachers, schools, and districts—often in front of the public. NCLB did not invent this view, but accelerated it to a new level. Accountability has always played a key role in exemplary instruction, as it should. No matter how much time and energy we invest in a literacy program, it's logical for us to demonstrate that our students achieve success. On the other hand, the degree to which these tests are elevated and the decreased emphasis on other forms of assessment is illogical. There's a distinction between accountability to promote responsiveness and that of standardized tests. While standardized tests *measure* accountability, informal day-to-day assessments help teachers identify students' strengths and needs in order to *achieve* accountability (Afflerbach 2007). That distinction must guide our thinking.

The International Reading Association provides important assessment standards (1994). It emphasizes that assessment must be designed to improve instruction, stating that the central function "is not to prove whether or not teaching or learning has taken place, but to improve the quality of teaching and learning" (11). This makes you an "assessment agent" since you possess invaluable knowledge about the literacy process and your students' progress in acquiring the necessary skills to become more proficient readers.

Defining the Terms: Summative and Formative Assessment

To understand RTI assessment, we must distinguish between summative and formative assessment. Standardized tests reflect summative assessment, while ongoing classroom data is an example of formative assessment. Summative can be described as assessment *of* students, while formative is assessment *for* students (Stiggins 2002; Edwards, Turner, and Mokhtari 2008). The chart provides a comparison.

SUMMATIVE ASSESSMENT	FORMATIVE ASSESSMENT
• Measures learning	• Improves learning
• Product-based	• Process-based
• An end goal in mind	• Conducted at key points
• Quantitative	• Qualitative
• Fixed	• Flexible
• Competitive	• Collaborative
• External (other)	• Internal (self-assessment)
• Instructional separation	• Instructional integration
• Focus on grade or score	• Focus on feedback

The lines between summative and formative assessment can be fuzzy. Some tools are labeled formative, but lean more toward labeling than informing what teachers might do next. In the end, it is the intent and timing of assessments that distinguish the purpose. Assessment is not formative simply because it occurs in a learning context. Worksheets are not formative since the intent is to secure a score rather than to help teachers gain insight that will lead to improved instruction. Wormeli (2006) reminds us that effective assessment must serve to *advance* learning rather than to simply *document* it (39).

Intent is an important point as we look at RTI, since many tools are described as formative despite evidence to the contrary. The intent of some progress monitoring tools is to judge learners and teachers rather than inform the next instructional step, making them summative. Formative assessment is not just about deciding whether instruction (or a package) is working, but to offer insights that translate to instruction. We must combine RTI data tools with assessments to more robustly support teaching and learning, or RTI may move from the "old stupid" to the "new stupid" (Hess 2009, 12).

The makers of standardized tests provide a warning. They emphasize that a single score cannot be used to make consequential judgments of teachers and schools, yet this is precisely what happens. Perhaps this warning is needed for RTI assessments, considering their demand on instructional time. If we spent less on RTI data collection tools, we would have a rich funding pool for differentiated resources and meaningful staff development. It seems that our priorities are seriously misplaced. The true test of how effective RTI will be rests largely on how thoughtfully assessment is addressed. We must carefully weigh the assessment proposed in RTI with those that are more directly correlated to high-quality instruction.

Organizing and Applying Varied Assessment Data

We can use data more efficiently and effectively by creating organizational systems that help us notice patterns of learning at deeper levels (Mokhtari, Rosemary, and Edwards 2008). Imagine the instructional benefits when data forms meaningful patterns we can use to promote new learning. Without such a system, data is a sea of meaningless numbers. Ultimately, it is what we do with and learn from data that is most important.

We must also ensure a balance of formative and summative assessment, a battle many are losing in RTI. Edwards, Turner, and Mokhtari (2008) explain: "There is an unfortunate imbalance between the call to account for what students learn and the need to create classroom conditions under which they can and should learn" (682). There is no substitute for authentic assessment that rises naturally from the learning process. Data that emerges from these experiences and the judgments teachers make to interpret and use that data is as "scientific" as that generated by any commercial test (Cambourne and Turbill 1990).

Assessment and instruction are simultaneous in that effective assessment activities are also worthwhile instructional activities (Wiggins 1992; Meyer 1992). This relationship is seamless; it's hard to tell where assessment stops and instruction begins. Quality data includes a rich pool of information. Of course, "being data rich doesn't necessarily translate into being data smart" (Reilly 2007, 770). We must supplement summative data with teacher observations, anecdotal records, discussion, retelling, think-alouds, self-evaluation, response writing, and learning samples we can document and analyze:

- What is the evidence that learning is or is not taking place?
- What does this evidence reflect about this child?
- What patterns are emerging that support a broader instructional view?
- How can we interpret the data to support this child's learning?
- How can we apply what we know about this child to instruction?
- What new evidence can we collect to demonstrate success?

Establishing an Instructional Assessment Cycle

Effective literacy assessment makes teaching more instructionally responsive and action-oriented, particularly if assessment taps all facets of learning. RTI data is often used to screen, or determine a child's response or nonresponse to instruction, rather than to teach. However, data that rises from the learning process can help us decide what to continue, modify, or alter in our instruction. We must question whether our RTI data consistently maintains the spirit of this essential process in theory *and* in practice.

An effective instructional model reflects a never-ending instruction-assessment cycle (see Figure 6.1). We continuously ask overarching questions about what the data reveals about our learners; the answers guide new instruction:

- Is there a problem?
- If so, what is the problem?
- In what ways might we address the problem?
- Is the instructional action resolving the problem?
- What adjustments might we need to make in the instruction?
- Did these instructional adjustments resolve the problem?

Using Varied Assessments to Complement and Extend RTI Data

The two main types of assessment in an RTI model are universal screening and progress monitoring. Universal screening is a schoolwide overview of student

Figure 6.1 The Instructional-Assessment Cycle

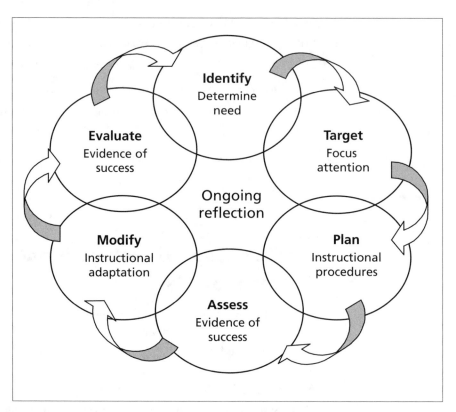

need related to grade level and district goals. Screening is not detailed enough to tell us *what* to teach; rather, it can only suggest *who* may need additional support beyond tier 1. Progress monitoring occurs throughout interventions with the intent to guide instruction. Simply put, screening is a single snapshot while progress monitoring is a series of snapshots during instruction.

Before we move to RTI assessment, we need to understand the supportive role of authentic classroom assessments. Let's consider information we can glean only from our authentic assessments using the following "windows of insight" on a child's reading:

- *Interests and attitudes about reading.* For example, Deandre is a sports enthusiast who literally devours anything related to the NBA. His struggle as a reader seems to dissipate when reading texts about his hero, Michael Jordan.

- *Strategy use across texts and contexts.* For example, Daniel has a wide range of effective strategies for narrative texts, but his struggle is glaringly obvious with factual texts. Limited exposure to content-area texts has left him with few tools for comprehending them.

- *Accessing prior knowledge and experiences.* For example, Marta lacks many of the life experiences that other children can draw upon to support reading. She benefits from supportive scaffolds that lay the foundation for new learning.

- **The role of peer collaboration.** For example, Todd excels when he can work in heterogeneous settings first, using learning that focuses on topics of interest. Rich conversations that revolve around peer engagement experiences set the stage for what follows.

- **Coping mechanisms based on emotional factors.** For example, Carlee has learned how to answer explicit questions common in basal texts. She needs help responding to questions for deeper levels of understanding.

- **Development as self-regulated learners.** For example, James has never been given the tools for independent learning. He possesses the skills to complete reinforcing seatwork activities, but he needs guidance in how to work independently.

- **The use of compensatory strategies.** For example, Melissa has limited recall of reading, but she responds positively to simple techniques. Visual literacy skills such as drawing and webbing have given her a way to remember key information.

- **Consolidation of new learning.** For example, Tyrone has not learned study strategies that will support learning. Simple approaches such as note taking, skimming, or rereading would support meaning and recall.

- **Ability to make up for other areas of deficit.** For example, Codie's numerous ear infections have made it hard for him to hear the sounds in words. However, strategies that draw on his strong visual memory such as memory games and flash cards resulted in a large bank of sight words. He is struggling to hear the sounds in words but has a strong visual memory that will support learning.

- **The use of sequential steps or tasks.** For example, Austin is not successful at most reading tasks because he has difficulty reading directions with several steps. He needs to learn how to read and understand multiple step-by-step directions.

- **Specific areas of "giftedness."** For example, Donisha is a talented artist who is constantly sketching pictures. This strength offers a bridge to reading as she can sketch her ideas and use her drawings as a concrete reference for learning.

- **Emotional issues.** For example, Jude performs very poorly on tests because he has developed a test phobia. He would benefit by learning test-taking strategies and relaxation techniques. In the meantime, tests do not reflect his capabilities.

- **The home–school connection.** For example, Thomas is not coping well with his parent's impending divorce. Turmoil at home has extended to school.

We can respond to limited home support with less homework and more in-school support.

- ***Poor teaching (perhaps the most challenging factor).*** For example, Kendall's previous teachers focused exclusively on letter-by-letter analysis devoid of meaning. She can read the words, but rarely understands what she reads. Accelerated support is now essential.

The richness of the RTI assessment process depends largely on what tools are used, how they are used, and whether these other, richer forms of observation and assessment are included. The quality of these tools, teachers' understanding of their purposes, and the frequency with which assessment occurs are all important variables. We must guard against assessment that supersedes and interferes with the instructional process. Often too much emphasis is placed on numerical values and too little on establishing a productive relationship between assessment and instruction.

The RTI View of Universal Screening: Reflections, Cautions, and Considerations

Universal screening occurs at key points, generally three times a year. Initial screening performed at the beginning of the year is often referred to as a benchmark since it is the first view of students' overall achievement. To use a GPS analogy, it reflects where the journey begins. The midyear and final checkpoints help teachers assess the impact of instruction throughout the year. Four key considerations must be addressed to ensure a multi-angle view of screening: the tool, screening schedule, who should conduct the screening, and interpretation of results.

Key Consideration 1: Choose a Universal Screening Tool

Currently, many universal screening devices are available. Most schools select from a rapidly growing number of commercial tools, although some create their own using state and district guidelines. Many schools must select from a "blessed" list of tools or screening devices that have been given a stamp of approval, often tools that have roots in NCLB and Reading First. Teachers are rarely given a voice in this selection, even though they and their students are the most impacted by the decision.

Screening devices are selected for many reasons—reasons that often have little to do with quality. For example, some are chosen by how quickly they can be administered rather than how well they align with curriculum goals or promote effective literacy. The time constraints associated with schoolwide screening are a factor, but we must also question the value of the tool itself. Several popular tools have become entrenched in the screening process, but their inherent value may be highly questionable.

Unfortunately, few schools begin with the critical selection criteria—what it means to be a proficient reader. The first step should be to articulate beliefs about teaching reading and valued aspects of the curriculum. A screening tool should reflect the literacy performances that are most valued. If we focus on performances that rely heavily on the rate of reading, this suggests that we value reading fast, particularly if numerical scores are emphasized. If we focus exclusively on oral reading performance, this reflects that oral reading is valued over silent reading. Too many schools are passionate about their values, but use screening tools in direct opposition. We must ensure that our practices emerge from our beliefs and values. We can't have it both ways.

Screening tools may be administered to individuals, small groups, or whole classes, by a person or via computer. Most devices are relatively fast, generally under ten minutes per student. This is particularly important with three testing intervals. Screening tools can be repeated at each interval and entered into a computerized data management system. This allows schools to view data within and across classrooms and schools for a comparative view across years. Data is usually fairly easy to access and view in a variety of ways for a quick visual reference. One note of caution: because they reflect grade-level assessments, screening tools rarely offer the kind of diagnostic information necessary to adjust instruction to the correct reading levels.

Screening may vary by grade to target specific skills. Early literacy skills such as alphabet recognition and sound awareness are assessed in kindergarten, while oral reading fluency is emphasized by the middle of first grade. Some schools use a cloze procedure in the later grades as a comprehension measure. A cloze procedure provides a text with missing words that students must "supply." This is then scored based on the precise accuracy of the word choice. In many cases, students who provide a missing word with one that preserves meaning may be penalized.

Packaged assessment has become a financial gold mine for publishers. The number of them seems to grow by leaps and bounds, each company promising an ideal screening tool. The best we can hope for is to find a tool that quickly identifies students who *may* need support in or beyond tier 1. Universal screening is a quick overview of skills, so the results are not specific enough to inform instruction. Without our day-to-day, informal assessment, screening is a narrow device. This is alarming considering the potential consequences of these assessments as they are used in RTI.

> *A* screening tool should reflect the literacy performances that are most valued.

YELLOW

Key Consideration 2: Establish a Universal Screening Schedule

The schedule created for universal screening must be constant from year to year. A consistent schedule allows for more accurate comparison within and across grades and schools. Some schools conduct screening monthly. This is discouraged since it significantly cuts into instructional time with little payoff. We must maintain a cautious balance between testing and instruction, particularly since progress monitoring adds to the demands once interventions are initiated. I have been in some schools where teachers were required to complete two assessments that took as much as three weeks. Multiply this by three and you begin to see why this is an irresponsible use of time. We must not allow any assessment device to substitute for high-quality instruction.

The screening schedule should follow simple guidelines. *Initial screening will not occur until two to three weeks after school begins.* This allows time to initiate informal assessments and build a community of learners. Informal assessments can be used in combination with screening to create a rich assessment pool. *The midyear screening occurs one to two weeks after the holiday break in January* to give students and teachers time to settle back into school. *Final screening occurs no later than two weeks before the end of the year* to make room for other priorities and end the year on a positive note.

Schools must establish a narrow testing window to minimize lost instructional time. Assessment must support rather than supplant instruction, so every effort should be made to complete screening in two to three days. With planning and coordination, this is realistic. Instructional assistants can monitor classrooms as teachers complete testing. This is particularly effective if teachers plan reinforcing activities such as read-alouds, shared and independent reading and discussion. Testing cannot compromise instructional time we can never retrieve.

Key Consideration 3: Identify the Individual to Conduct Screening

The person responsible for instruction has the most to gain from conducting assessments. When you consider the consequences of testing, it doesn't make sense for anyone besides the teacher to assume this role. I have been in countless schools where teachers have no direct hand in testing. They are given a spreadsheet of numerical data and asked to make crucial decisions. Numbers *do* lie if other factors are not taken into consideration. The data is less important than what we choose to do with that data after it is collected. This requires teacher involvement.

Moreover, some of the most crucial information we can glean comes from observing students in the context of testing. Invaluable clues can be gained from observing the reading process, but these are visible solely to a tester who understands what to listen and watch for. Numbers rarely reveal this critical information. For example, consider the important observations that arise from these questions:

- Does the child appear uncomfortable or confident?
- Does the child pause at unknown words or actively search for information?
- Does the child appeal to the teacher frequently or use strategies independently?
- Does the child make miscues and read on, or reread to self-correct?
- Does the child ever look ahead or reread to get back on track?

We cannot afford to delegate screening—we must own it. Too many schools remove this powerful internal informant by assigning testing responsibility to others. Some schools have support staff conduct testing while teachers continue instruction. Some hire outside testing support or initiate what is referred to as a SWAT team. Using this approach, district personnel converge on the school to conduct testing. These approaches are justified by emphasizing that they reduce lost teaching time and that teachers are less objective, making unbiased testers preferable.

These are not logical arguments. The issue of teacher bias is easily addressed with clear guidelines and staff development. Professional development can help teachers understand how to use hidden sources of information and integrate this knowledge into teaching. The benefits of teacher as tester far outweigh any disadvantages, considering the wealth of valuable information we glean from testing. Professional development that builds a deeper understanding of screening and its interpretation is no more costly than hiring outsiders, and far more productive in the long run.

We further remove the teacher from the assessment process when teachers combine classes and are responsible for one curriculum area with multiple classes. In this approach, teachers trade students so one teacher teaches reading all day while the other teaches science and social studies. In some schools, teachers assigned to reading are responsible for testing both classes. Imagine the frustration that ensues. More important, imagine the depth of knowledge we lose if we spend only half the time allotted with students. This is a highly questionable approach, both from an assessment *and* instructional standpoint.

Some schools view teacher as tester as a gradual process of compromise. These schools use support staff for the initial screening while teachers engage in staff development; teachers are then responsible for subsequent assessments. Some schools use support staff the first year; then teachers assume the role in the second year with continued support. This approach is certainly better than taking teachers entirely out of the loop, but it seems that a better approach is to provide training *before* RTI is implemented. Administrators often overlook the value of information gathered during the screening and assessment process.

Key Consideration 4: Interpret the Universal Screening Results

Each commercial screening tool comes with detailed guidelines, so I will not offer recommendations here. Universal screening explores general grade-level reading skills at three intervals. Initial screening identifies those students who may not be successful with grade-level curriculum so support can be offered immediately. It also identifies classrooms with an inordinate number of students at risk. The next two intervals monitor student progress and explore the effectiveness of a general education program. If this growth is not reflected for all students, including those deemed at risk, the classroom teacher may need help differentiating instruction to meet varying needs.

One of the most important questions schools must address is how to place equal focus on qualitative and quantitative data. Test results are often recorded in a data management system and teachers are given a visual display of scores. Companies argue that measures included on screening devices are supported by research. This may be true for some test features, but companies fail to address the relevance of a single source of information to the exclusion of others. This leads to misinterpretation. How do you analyze a spreadsheet when only one measure is represented numerically?

For example, most screening includes oral reading fluency. There is no question that most proficient readers demonstrate more fluent reading than those who struggle; Fluency almost always results in higher levels of comprehension. Comprehension and fluency are connected, but emphasis on speed over qualities such as expression, phrasing, or inflection is problematic. Worse, the comprehension portion of some popular tools seems almost an afterthought. One must wonder how counting the number of words in a retelling translates to comprehension. Selecting assessments that more closely approximate reading is one way to make the process more robust. One example is running records in which the student is assessed in the process of reading; teachers analyze strategy use and assess comprehension both during and after the reading.

This emphasis on analysis of oral reading is critical. Teachers gain a great deal of information beyond scores by exploring the reading or thinking process before, during, and after reading, yet we fail to emphasize this point strongly enough. Analysis of oral reading that focuses exclusively on numerical scores has limited ability to make crucial decisions, considering three identical scores often reflect different needs. These needs can be determined only by closer inspection and analysis. The same oral reading score might suggest weakness in word analysis, vocabulary, fluency, comprehension, independent strategy use, or even attention. One number doesn't tell all.

These tools also fail to take into account many variables that impact scores, such as the background knowledge of students, the use of specialized vocabulary, the level of readability, sentence structure, dialect, text structure, or familiarity with genre. Moreover, the results fail to consider other equally important aspects of the learning process, such as nervousness or emotions that always make their way into testing. Only knowledgeable and observant teachers who are sensitive to these factors can determine their importance.

Universal screening provides a quick glance of general grade-level reading skills, but it is not a comprehensive test, as emphasized by Routman (2008): "Combined with formative assessments, summative assessments can help improve instruction and learning. By themselves, summative assessments do not provide a comprehensive picture of a child's achievement" (80). Informal data paints a much broader instructional canvas. Reilly (2007) describes using "pockets of learning" or seemingly insignificant moments in the day that inform teaching. Informal assessment occurs as teachers observe students engaged in literacy events, confer with them about reading and writing, ask students to verbalize their own thinking, use learning samples such as portfolios over time, or engage students in self-assessment. Waiting to conduct screening until a few weeks after the start of the school year gives teachers time to access these critical forms of assessment, which will support what universal screening can reveal.

Case studies can be integrated with professional development as an effective way to help teachers understand more subtle findings than most assessment yields. Actual assessment samples—informal and formal—are used for problem solving to better understand the testing process. This is an effective context for professional learning because teachers can use authentic student samples to generate questions, problem solve for instructional goals, and relate this to their own instructional practices. Professional learning experiences rooted in practice are powerful.

Informal data paints a much broader instructional canvas.

The RTI View of Progress Monitoring: Reflections, Cautions, and Considerations

Progress monitoring is a key RTI assessment tool for determining response to intervention. The term is literal in that data will monitor student progress throughout instruction. To use the GPS analogy, progress monitoring provides the turn-by-turn directions that guide the journey along a projected path, with road signs and markers along the way as evidence of success, "recalculating" to continuously move toward effective instruction. We can see where the journey begins (baseline), each stop along the way (performance over time), and the final destination (expected rate of growth). The same four key considerations discussed for screening must be addressed to ensure a multi-angle view of progress monitoring.

Key Consideration 1: Choose a Progress Monitoring Tool

Progress monitoring tools are aligned to instruction, and unlimited options are available from the same companies that offer screening. These generally incorporate the five pillars: phonemic awareness, phonics, fluency, vocabulary, and comprehension. The most common tools emphasize early literacy or oral reading, with new assessments continuously added. A rapidly growing supply of screening tools makes it challenging to distinguish effective tools from those that are ineffective.

Progress monitoring is individual assessment collected throughout instruction, so a relatively quick tool is important. Curriculum-based measurement (CBM) is commonly used. These one-minute probes generally reflect how much (number) or how long (time), using a graphic to view growth over time. The intent of progress monitoring is to support decision making such as whether to continue, change, or adjust instruction. One or two indicators are selected for interventions, so the tool must match what is being taught.

The dilemma of progress monitoring is twofold. First, the quick nature of the test decreases the richness of information. Second, some of the most popular tools have a limited scope, such as a heavy focus on speed over prosodic features of language or the accuracy of oral reading. Most emphasize quantitative or numerical data over qualitative assessment of the reading process since they capture a brief sample. This makes it easy to misinterpret or apply a narrow view. Worse, the role of silent reading is often ignored.

It has been has suggested that RTI should refer to response to *instruction* (Farstrup 2007; Allington 2008). Progress monitoring can move us to the dangerous waters where RTI becomes *response to assessment*. There is always the risk that the data collection process will overpower rather than support instruction. Our priority should be to collect data that yields high-quality information for instructional purposes rather than a mere window dressing of student progress. Do students read faster because we promote speed with minimal gain in understanding? Do students learn word lists they are unable to apply in connected texts? Do students identify pseudo-words and make up words in real reading? These are all legitimate questions we must ask in a multi-angle view of RTI. What we assess may be a tradeoff for what we need to teach.

It isn't hard to create a closer connection between authentic instruction and data collection. You can easily photocopy a specific text and use it as an assessment protocol. Use this text to code oral reading directly on the page by marking miscues and self-corrections. Oral reading strategies, vocabulary, and sight word knowledge are assessed via meaningful text rather than isolated word lists. This makes any text a source for progress monitoring that more closely approximates instruction. We can amass tremendous knowledge about the reading process in the context of reading and save the time and cost of securing commercial tools with detailed scoring procedures.

Comprehension can be measured more effectively with a simple framework for questions using QAR (question-answer relationships) as a guide (Raphael 1986; Raphael, Highfield, and Au 2006). Ask or generate questions that reflect the QAR categories: In-the-Book Questions (Right There; Think and Search); In-My-Head Questions (Author and You; On My Own). You can create a simple rubric to secure a numerical score that will provide a more authentic measure of the relationship between assessment and instruction than a number alone.

Current progress monitoring tools often muddy this relationship with stilted passages. Assessments that mirror the very performances you are exploring are the most effective tools. The more those assessments "mirror a view of the kind of readers we are trying to grow, the more useful they will be" (Wallis 2009, 105). The further these tools remove assessment from instruction, the less valuable they are. In other words, *assessment rooted in real reading events leads to improved instruction*. Companies selling tools grow richer as the quality of instruction suffers.

Key Consideration 2: Establish a Progress Monitoring Schedule

Establishing a schedule for progress monitoring is complicated since it occurs with interventions and varies with each tier. Data collection for progress monitoring is closely tied to instruction, so it has a multifunctional purpose—to establish where students begin, identify expected growth, and measure performance over time. Data is generally recorded on a graph for a quick visual record of learning throughout instruction.

The instructional intensity of each tier determines the frequency of assessment, and thus scheduling. This means progress monitoring is conducted more often at tier 2 than tier 1 and more often at tier 3 than tier 2. These adjustments allow us to monitor according to student need. Realistic guidelines are needed to ensure that we do not interrupt the instruction that data is meant to support, thus robbing instructional time from students who can least afford it.

Scheduling recommendations for data collection range from weekly to monthly at tier 1, three times weekly to every two weeks at tier 2, and daily to every two weeks at tier 3. There is general agreement that monitoring frequency increases with instructional intensity, so a sliding scale of data collection makes sense. On the other hand, it also makes sense to guard against lost instructional time with a "less is more" mentality.

The argument about the frequency of progress monitoring cannot be one-sided and address only the data collection some deem appropriate. We must emphasize that assessment accompanies *every* learning activity, regardless of where instruction occurs. Tier 3 assessment complements tier 1 assessment and vice versa as we dramatically expand the assessment viewpoint. Assessment that occurs minute by minute and day by day in the context of learning provides a far more valuable view than one-minute probes.

Key Consideration 3: Identify the Individual to Conduct Progress Monitoring

Identifying who conducts progress monitoring is an easy question since it occurs throughout instruction. Instruction and assessment are inseparably intertwined, so the interventionist should always collect the data. This allows us to incorporate other measures that are visible only in the context of assessment—or how students behave during the test. We can also generate data when we probe for more information: Tell me more. What do you mean? What makes you think so? How did you figure that out? What might you need to do next?

Some schools build time into the day for teachers to collect data—using a rotating schedule, instructional assistants relieve teachers for this purpose. I agree with the intent since instructional time is sacred, but we are simply stealing time from a different place in the day. Five minutes seems inconsequential, but this is almost enough time for an additional instructional session by the end of the week. It makes more sense to embed informal assessment into the instructional process with less focus on numerical probes.

The demand for progress monitoring leads to other implications. If the teacher is struggling to keep up with progress monitoring, there's a danger this may substitute for classroom assessment embedded in authentic instruction. We can't afford to ignore these valuable day-to-day assessments such as observing, conferring, and using running records to inform instructional planning. This leads us to reduce learning to numerical values recorded on a graph with inaccurate conclusions and to abandon the very assessments that would allow us to intelligently and responsibly differentiate instruction.

We can't afford to ignore these valuable day-to-day assessments such as observing, conferring, and using running records to inform instructional planning.

Key Consideration 4: Interpret the Progress Monitoring Results

Companies that provide progress monitoring tools detail the collection and scoring process, so I will simply provide an overview of some key points. *Interpreting assessment is likely to be the most challenging aspect of RTI;* schools must take every step to maintain the value of the process so it supports rather than substitutes for instruction. If progress monitoring is used cautiously and flexibly, it *can* inform the instructional process. This depends on several factors: focus of assessment, quality of tools, method of interpretation, and complementary assessments. We must ensure that the data we collect is worth evaluating or progress monitoring can become an enormous waste of time.

Progress monitoring celebrates the idea that a picture is worth a thousand words. Data is graphed to provide a visual illustration of where students began (baseline), where we want them to go (targetline), and performance over time (trendline). Criteria are established to determine entry and exit points using a slope of progress. If the slope of the line indicates an expected rate of progress, it means that instruction is working. A sharp upward movement may indicate that support is no longer required. A downward slope signals that a major instructional adjustment is needed.

I often hear in conversations about education that "hunches" are out and data is in. The graph I just described is designed to visually array data as "proof." I advise we get away from the either-or stance, and stop pitting research against practitioner's hunches. As Malcolm Gladwell showed in his book *Blink*, neuroscience and psychology findings point to the idea that brilliant decision makers are not those that process the most data, but those who are good at "thin slicing—filtering the very few factors that matter from an overwhelming number of variables" (Gladwell 2007).

We need the thin slicing talents of teachers to catch the conflict between what numbers may suggest and what they actually mean. For example, two students with identical fluency scores may need very different instruction. Does the score suggest that instruction should address fluency, sight word knowledge, or oral language? Is the oral reading fluency score low because students do not have an adequate store of sight words, are not using visual information, or do not have sufficient background knowledge for this text?

The emphasis on oral reading to the exclusion of silent reading is also worth noting, particularly beyond the early grades. Oral reading samples may paint inaccurate pictures for students who read silently with understanding but struggle when they read orally. On the other hand, a good oral reading score may miss those students who read silently with little understanding. Progress monitoring gets complicated if instruction emphasizes silent reading comprehension but assessments focus on oral reading—a definite mismatch.

It cannot be emphasized too often that progress monitoring reflects only one form of assessment. It can't replace equally valuable assessments that may more appropriately support decision making. And stakes are high when we consider decisions that rise from this data. Informal assessment and evaluation complement progress monitoring. This may begin with professional hunches that are transformed into hypotheses that lead to solid data support. As stated by Johnston and Costello (2005), "It is not just what gets assessed, but how it is assessed that has implications for how it is learned" (256).

Acknowledging Dilemmas, Challenges, and Limitations of RTI Assessment

There are many factors to consider as we put RTI assessments in place. We must openly explore the benefits and potential pitfalls that abound. Testing is not a perfect science, so we must avoid privileging any single instrument to make critical decisions about students. This overview of key points will help us create a more thoughtful plan.

The Use of Data to Guide Instructional Decisions

The dipstick is an ingenious tool. I just pull it out, stick it in, and pull it out again. In seconds, it assesses my car's oil needs. It's quick. It's simple. It's *fairly* reliable. Occasionally the final analysis is fuzzy since I can't tell if I need quart of oil or whether oil slid onto the dipstick on the way out. No bells ring. No lights flash. I must interpret the final analysis. I'm not criticizing the dipstick, as it works great for the job it's designed to do. It's just that it is incapable of doing more. I need to use other information, such as how my car drives or advice from those with far more "dipstick smarts" than I possess.

The same reservations should be applied to one- to ten-minute snippets of data. Like my dipstick, they are quick, simple, fairly accurate—and limited in scope. Lipson and Wixson (2008) state, "If progress is monitored on only one or two dimensions of reading, then these one or two things will become the most important focus for instruction, at the expense of other equally important components" (5). We must be sensitive observers of learning (Clay 2006) who are present in an instructional process that is visible and audible (Johnston 2005). We must include day-to-day happenings to notice, document, and purposefully use evidence of learning.

The Impact on Instructional Time

The ticking clock is the biggest obstacle of RTI data collection. The magnitude of screening and ongoing progress monitoring along with other testing obligations can be considerable and can easily overpower the instructional process. We can't add time to the day, so lost instructional time is inevitable. Sixty seconds multiplies if we assess as often as recommended. The time required to assess, record, graph, and analyze results for every student is not insignificant. Any discussions that revolve around RTI assessment must address the impact on instructional time.

The sad truth, I am finding, is that the first thing to go is the most informative day-to-day assessment, which teachers are abandoning in exasperation. We need reasonable schedules that do not turn teaching into testing and exclude other far richer instructional informants, or the loss of instructional time will be catastrophic. This is a particularly dangerous compromise for students who are already lagging behind. We must react responsibly or RTI will intensify the existing testing culture tenfold.

We need reasonable schedules that do not turn teaching into testing and exclude other far richer instructional informants, or the loss of instructional time will be catastrophic.

The Critical Role of Ownership

Professional development is the only way to allow teachers to assume ownership of assessment. This is not about how to use assessment packages but how to adopt a broader view of assessment within and beyond RTI. What can data really tell us? What are the limitations of data? What student behaviors inform the testing process? What informal assessments support data? How can we more deeply analyze the instructional process? How can we translate data into instruction? Responding to these questions openly provides consistent information in a supportive environment with ongoing guidance.

We can maximize teacher ownership by establishing professional learning partnerships. When teachers observe one another as they are engaged in these experiences, they benefit from a rich learning opportunity as well as second set of eyes and ears "for overcoming the limitations of their own assessment lens" (Johnston 2005, 74). These partnerships build internal systems of shared collaboration and feedback. This is particularly effective if coaches or reading specialists offer insight throughout this process.

Meeting the Challenge of RTI Assessment

Will assessment in an RTI model be challenging? Without a doubt! Will it be worth the effort? The answer is that assessment is a double-edged sword. Assessment can easily get out of hand, and students and teachers will pay the price. If we proceed cautiously and maintain a flexible view, it *will* be worth the effort. If we don't, the damage to quality instruction is irrevocable. We must design assessment in an RTI model in such a way that we can ensure children get the learning experiences they need and deserve.

Teachers are clearly responding to increased demands for testing. The National Commission on Teaching and America's Future estimates that one-third of new teachers leave after three years, and 46 percent within five years. As quoted in *NEA Today* (Kopkowski 2008), commission president Tom Carroll compares it to "continually dumping sand into a bucket with holes in the bottom." Teachers cite reasons such as a lack of administrative or district support, growing NCLB testing requirements, and the need to do more in less time. I fear RTI in its current assessment design will multiply this number once full-scale implementation begins—and veteran teachers won't be far on their heels.

RTI will be successful only if we establish a broader view of assessment that will inform teaching without controlling it. We must question the quality of every assessment tool we use and refuse any instrument proposed simply because it's popular or easy. This requires ongoing dialogue and generating and responding to many questions:

- What do we want to assess?
- What tools will help us do that?
- How can we look more deeply at student performances?
- How can we enrich RTI assessments with more authentic assessment forms?

- What professional development is needed for teachers to be effective?
- How can we offer ongoing professional support?

If we are too busy looking for the ideal commercial assessment package, we may ignore the real purpose of assessment: to support and measure student learning. Judy Wallis draws on the wonderful feeling of sitting by a campfire as a metaphor for effective assessment, stating, "Imagine if teachers considered the individual and collective growth of their students in authentic ways where the learner was placed at the center. Imagine if we balanced mandated tests with a collection of thoughtfully conceived tools to communicate progress and to provide direction" (2009, 96).

RTI places educators in a unique locale. We've arrived at a dangerous crossroad between choosing literacy assessments that are inseparably connected to instruction and those that impinge upon the very instruction they are intended to support. If RTI has any hope of flourishing, we will need to be careful about the assessment path we take. At some point, professional knowledge and personal responsibility will surely prevail, and we will turn away from the path leading down a dark and frightening road and opt for the one that leads to Wallis' assessment campfire. Imagine indeed!

CHAPTER 7

Maximizing the Success Factors:

Making RTI Work Schoolwide

> *A* garden requires patient labor and attention. Plants do not grow
> merely to satisfy ambitions or to fulfill good intentions. They thrive
> because someone expended effort on them.
>
> —*Liberty Hyde Bailey*

Full-scale implementation of RTI will undoubtedly be challenging. The multi-angle view I have proposed calls for schools to adopt a broad perspective that acknowledges the critical role of teachers. The following ten key points summarize what we must do as we use the multi-angle view to *make RTI work*.

1. ***Do your homework first to set the stage for success.***

   RTI is too important to initiate haphazardly. Thoughtful reflection and a detailed plan of action are needed *before* implementation—awareness is the first step (Lipson and Wixson 2008). Create an RTI framework to support your school given existing resources and build the necessary skill sets so teachers won't flounder when confusions arise (and they will). Farstrup (2008) states, "Teachers at all levels need to be fully informed as to the opportunities and pitfalls that RTI presents" (21).

2. *Secure the resources that will support differentiated literacy at all tiers.*

   RTI will be successful only if we make a commitment to high-quality resources within and across tiers. In the end, this is a question of establishing priorities—we can refuse low-level packages and opt for more responsive and responsible choices. Carefully evaluate and select assessments and offer a range of resources to move teachers beyond a "grade-level box." Will you use funding on whole-group class texts and consumable workbooks or emphasize small-group sets of high-quality texts across the curriculum for placement in a central book room? Our choices reflect how serious we are about literacy success for all students or whether we are merely giving lip service to differentiation.

3. *Expand the research parameters to yield a broader knowledge base.*

   Until we redefine a broader view of "evidence-based research," I fear that a rich body of research will be systematically whittled away in lieu of mandated and packaged teaching. RTI should not tell teachers what to think; rather it should suggest *what they might think about* given *all* existing research. A broader knowledge base requires us to explore how this rich research can be translated to more effective teaching. It also requires us to ensure that teachers are not simply complying with the directives of a lesson plan but reflectively translating those suggestions to students who rarely fit a cookie-cutter approach to teaching and learning.

4. *Acknowledge the role of expert teachers in the RTI instructional process.*

   There is no substitute for expert teachers in the RTI model. We must support *every* teacher's efforts to work diligently toward greater expertise and proficiency to ensure that all students receive high-quality literacy instruction. As a national consultant, I am saddened when educators who care deeply about students are offered minimal training and support to take these steps. Too often teachers are told to use a packaged approach or criticized when they attempt to veer off the beaten path. We must foster an atmosphere of professional curiosity and reflection that provides every teacher with a professional learning environment of inquiry, support, and feedback.

5. *Build a solid foundation for a stronger framework.*

The trickle-up effect makes tier 1 the first order of business. If tier 1 intervention is not based on high-quality literacy, a flawed basic system will become the foundation for everything that follows. This is like expecting a house with a weak foundation to hold steady at the first blast of wind. If struggling readers have access to appropriate texts and tasks only at higher tiers, RTI is not likely to reduce the number of students who struggle. Allington (2008) states, "Most struggling readers never catch up with their higher-achieving classmates because schools create school days for them where they struggle all day long" (1). We cannot "expect students to adjust to the learning when the learning should really be adjusted to the learner" (Gregory and Chapman 2006, 2). This is not a thirty-minute proposition; targeting student needs matters all day, every day.

6. *Strengthen the coordination between tiers using a fluid design.*

A multitiered RTI model requires a system of coordinated supports so that each tier is an extension of those that precede or follow it. The needs of students do not change simply because they move from one tier to another. Professionals at each support tier should work hand-in-hand to accommodate these needs across tiers. Guidelines are established for each tier, but this must be based on a flexible design that creates tiers that are inseparable. Professional collaboration is critical for coordination and integration of tiers. We cannot cut corners on this point.

7. *Make interventions more "intervention-like."*

Cooper, Chard, and Kiger state that an intervention is designed to "prevent or stop failure with instruction beyond what is provided in the classroom program" (2006, 13). Interventions offer *more* to meet the specific need of students with accelerated instruction that emphasizes skills and strategies within the context of reading. Interventions must match students' reading level using texts reflecting a gradient of difficulty that can be adjusted by increasing the text challenges to accommodate the students' changing needs. As students become more proficient readers, more complex texts are provided with guidance and feedback, but always those that are within the child's reach. Interventions are not isolated skills, but teacher-supported experiences using engaging texts. In short, an intervention immerses students in the very literacy experiences we are trying to promote.

8. *Highlight professional development with a scaffolded system of support.*

   Professional development is purposefully discussed throughout this book because it's an essential but too often ignored success factor. Professional differentiation allows us to adjust these experiences to meet the needs of each teacher according to his or her level of understanding at that time. Dorn and Soffos (2001) highlight an important role of staff development, stating: "The goal is a self-regulated teacher who recognizes the capacity of her knowledge for guiding, monitoring and reflecting on her own progress" (89). Effective schools apply an apprenticeship model to professional development as teachers assume an active role in their own learning with ongoing support (Dorn, French, and Jones 1998). If RTI has a chance of success, we must support teachers in building deeper levels of knowledge. Anything less is doomed to fail.

9. *Maximize the support of administrators through increased engagement.*

   The quality and form of school leadership is crucial to RTI success. Effective school leaders possess a rich knowledge base; they know what to look for, what strategies to promote, how to support top-notch instruction, and what resources can best do this. They assume an active role by learning alongside teachers in a positive climate of change with ongoing feedback. They are a visible presence in the learning process and encourage collaboration and reflective inquiry. They allow teachers to share confusions as well as successes in a supportive environment. They know what high-quality literacy looks like and promote it daily. For better or worse, teachers follow the lead of administrators, so this engagement is essential.

10. *Maintain a clear sense of purpose.*

    Many teachers lament that there is no single RTI model, but rigid directives could make the situation far worse by mandating poor quality or inflexible commercial programs that don't address students' needs. Establish shared beliefs and understandings first; *then create an RTI framework that nurtures those beliefs and understandings.* Unless we insist on creating a flexible framework that uses both published resources *and* teacher judgment, RTI will get lost in a financially profitable shuffle. Above all, RTI is about students and teachers. We must never lose sight of this.

Looking to the Future: Meeting the Promise of RTI

GREEN

Routman (2003) encourages us to "teach with a sense of urgency." The dictionary defines *urgency* as "pressing importance requiring speedy action." Kotter (2008) applies it to the business world as those who make the most of each work day by alleviating those activities that impede their goals in order to work faster and smarter. We must approach RTI the same way: by alleviating those things that impede our efforts and exploring how we can work smarter. The stakes are high, so this urgency is warranted.

Memories of small-town 1972 Missouri rush over me as I gather my closing thoughts of this book. Twelve students walked through a doorway and literally changed my life forever. I am grateful to have tasted the freedom of choice in those early days and even more grateful to students who allowed me to learn with and through them. I hope that this same freedom can be preserved in the RTI process. The RTI we deserve would have been a welcome companion in my passionate search for knowledge. Twelve struggling readers blossomed alongside a young, bright-eyed realist struggling to become a better teacher. How I wish I could thank them now.

I still recall the terror as I gazed at the editor's name on a scrap of paper. Since that day, I've spent countless sleepless nights struggling to put my hopes and fears for RTI on paper. One day when self-doubt was almost debilitating, John Mayer's song came on the radio. "Say" became my mantra as I began each day listening to words that propelled my fingers across the keyboard: *You better know that in the end it's better to say too much than never to say what you need to say.* I believe RTI has tremendous potential and that it will be worth the hard work and determination if we maintain a unified voice in a never-ending search for excellence. So in the end . . .

Say what you need to say.

BOOK STUDY GUIDE

Book Study Suggestions

Learning is inherently social. Though as teachers we sometimes feel isolated, most of us know the benefits of taking time to engage with colleagues. It is through these conversations, or "teacher talk" as Regie Routman calls it, that we clarify and enrich our own ideas. This is particularly true when new ideas, such as response to intervention, arise in education. While there are many ways to structure a study group, it is most important to foster a climate in which teachers feel they can participate freely and safely in the ongoing conversations and exchange of ideas. Other guidelines can make book study more productive. Here are a few things you might consider.

Watch group size: You may want to kick off discussion with a general question and then break into smaller groups. Often the optimal number is four or five to ensure there is time for all to exchange ideas. The larger group can reassemble at the end to debrief.

Use study questions: Some groups find it more comfortable to start with a few questions to get conversation going. There are various ways to use questions.

- Put three or four questions in an envelope and randomly pull them out for discussion.
- Create a chart with two or three starter questions; then ask the group to generate more, tapping participants' own personal interests and needs.
- Decide on three or four questions and divide the group according to participants' interest in those topics. This allows for more in-depth study.
- Make copies of the suggested questions for everyone and invite discussion without deciding where to start.

Create an agenda: Make sure you have planned a beginning and ending time and *always* honor those times. Teachers are busy, so knowing how long your meetings will last is important.

Stay focused on the topic: Plan a procedure that is transparent. You might start by saying something like, "Let's decide on a signal to use when we feel the discussion is drifting and then have everyone agree to help regain focus."

Include everyone: Keep groups small enough that even the quietest member is encouraged to speak. Active listening on everyone's part will help. Remember that periods of silence should be expected when people are thinking.

Share leadership: Rotate the role of discussion moderator. Identify several responsibilities of the moderator—for example, suggesting a big idea from a chapter or group of chapters, and synthesizing or summarizing at the end. Remember that in a study group, *everyone* is a learner. This isn't the place for an "expert."

Create a list of norms: Simple, transparent expectations often make study groups function more smoothly and increase potential for success. These might include some of the preceding suggestions, such as ways to invite a tentative member into the conversation, expectations about listening, start and stop times, and a procedure for refocusing.

Set dates for the next meeting: Always leave knowing when you will meet again and who will moderate the discussion.

Engage in reflection: Stop from time to time to reflect on what you are learning and how you might make your group's interactions more productive.

Celebrate learning: Make sure you take time to enjoy one another and celebrate your learning.

The following questions relate to the content in each chapter. Many more ideas and suggestions are presented in each chapter.

Chapter 1

The Paths Leading to the RTI Crossroads

1. Howard uses the term *internal radar* as a way to recognize important new ideas worth incorporating. What recent important ideas/research have you incorporated into your own teaching?

2. Do you agree that by intervening early, most students will read at grade level? How might this belief affect your teaching?

3. As you consider resources for RTI, what are some guidelines you use to guide and evaluate your choices?

4. Discuss the relative importance of the five pillars (phonemic awareness, phonics, fluency, vocabulary, and comprehension) the National Reading Panel report highlights, drawing on your own teaching experiences.

5. Some suggest the National Reading Panel report neglected to look at important research. What other areas/practices do you believe are important in the teaching of reading?

6. What kinds of grouping do you use in your own classroom? How do you decide on grouping structures?

7. How might you encourage and organize ways for teachers to collaborate and talk with one another to ensure increased student achievement?

Chapter 2

RTI: A Framework for Responsive Differentiated Teaching

1. If RTI initiatives focused more on creating exemplary instruction than on intervention, how might this build stronger literacy programs in your school?

2. As you consider the RTI framework, what differences do you see among the three tiers? Discuss students who you think might benefit at each tier.

3. Often the classroom teacher is left out during intervention planning and instructional delivery. Discuss why the teacher is integral to the success of struggling students.

4. Howard discusses the pros and cons of push-in versus pull-out intervention. Share your own thoughts and experiences with either or both.

5. Discuss the cycle of good teaching (Figure 2.2). How might using this cycle provide a process for improving instruction on your campus?

6. "Double dipping" is an interesting way of thinking about increased needs of struggling students. How would this concept help you better support your own struggling students?

7. Discuss how authentic assessment might offer greater insights about your students. What kids of assessments could you design that would grow out of students' day-to-day literacy instruction and experiences?

Chapter 3

Tier 1 Intervention: High-Quality Instruction for All

1. Consider the typical daily schedule included in the chapter. How does this schedule compare with your own? What changes might you consider in either schedule to increase students' access to high-quality literacy instruction?

2. Discuss read-aloud as an instructional practice. How might you use it with more effectiveness in your own classroom?

3. Howard references Tomlinson's work in suggesting that differentiation occurs in three ways: content, process, or product. Share your own experiences in differentiation using one or more of the three. What was the effect on students' learning?

4. Several ways to analyze students' reading are suggested in the chapter. What tools do you use to learn more about students' strengths and needs?

5. Leveling systems are often used to match students to texts. How does your school ensure teachers have access to a variety of levels and genres?

6. Whole-to-part instruction is an important concept for all learners. Discuss why it is particularly important for struggling students.

7. The gradual release of responsibility model is an important concept in RTI. How do you ensure that students have adequate modeling and support before they perform independently?

8. Howard discusses Allington's "six Ts" of exemplary instruction. Offer some examples for each from your own instruction.

Chapter 4

Tier 2 Intervention: Establishing a Coordinated Continuum of Support

1. Consider Nikolai's three questions. How can you use these questions to guide your own teaching?

2. How does using common language and strategies increase the potential for student success and achievement?

3. Think of your own "Codie stories." Share how your careful efforts made a difference for the student.

4. Consider your own resources—do you have an adequate supply of high-quality texts to support students with varied needs? How might you improve your instructional collection?

5. How might you ensure the *quality* of time spent in monitoring student progress?

6. Teachers often learn improved instructional practices from colleagues. How will you incorporate ways for teachers to share their expertise?

7. Howard discusses the need for expert intervention. How might you use the expertise in your school to provide the highest-quality intervention?

8. Howard lists a number of ways to increase instructional intensity. Discuss the list and ways you have incorporated or how you might incorporate these practices into your own teaching.

9. Using the analogy of slicing a pie, think about your own classroom instruction. How do you "slice the pie" and what changes, if any, might you consider making in your own division of time?

10. Consider the "less is more" concept. What might you eliminate to make room for more robust practices?

Chapter 5

Tier 3 Intervention: Intensifying the Instructional Support

1. What process will you put in place to decide who will deliver tier 3 instruction in your school?

2. Think of a time when you struggled with an idea or skill and someone supported your learning. In what ways did the "teacher" scaffold you? What was the effect of that scaffolding?

3. Buly and Valencia found that students who did not pass state-mandated tests had different instructional needs. Discuss how these differences might call for different instructional interventions.

4. Consider the three RTI tiers, each designed to address students' needs. How can your school ensure that all students receive high-quality instruction initially so that the tiers are used to support students who are truly struggling?

5. The concept of continuous assessment is critical in RTI planning. How might it be used to adjust teaching and plan necessary support?

Chapter 6

Broadening the Role of Assessment in an RTI Model

1. Discuss the difference between summative and formative assessment. Share some examples of each that your school uses to monitor students' learning.

2. Howard lists some of the insights teachers learn from authentic assessments. Discuss these using examples from your own teaching.

3. Screening tools play an important role in RTI. How can you ensure these "tools" yield helpful information that pinpoints students' instructional needs?

4. What professional development might teachers need to ensure less bias in testing and more productive uses of assessment data?

5. What kinds of progress monitoring tools might your school add to gain greater information about students' strengths and needs?

6. How can you help ensure a healthy balance between instruction and assessment in your school?

7. Howard introduces some shortcomings of progress monitoring tools. Discuss how these might compromise students' access to quality instruction.

8. How might a "broader view of assessment" affect your school's assessment practices?

Chapter 7

Maximizing the Success Factors:
Making RTI Work Schoolwide

1. Consider Howard's ten success factors for RTI. What key points does your school need to address to ensure success?

2. What additional resources should your school consider budgeting for to make RTI implementation successful?

3. Coordination among the tiers is essential for student success. What support might your school create to ensure this coordination and timely action on students' behalf?

4. Consider the possibilities of RTI and the potential pitfalls. How will your school avoid the pitfalls to create a strong successful model?

5. Using the key points, reflect on a realistic schedule for accomplishing these things.

REFERENCES

Afflerbach, P. 2007. *Understanding and Using Reading Assessment K–2*. Newark, DE: International Reading Association.

Afflerbach, P., P. D. Pearson, and S. G. Paris. 2008. "Clarifying Differences Between Reading Skills and Reading Strategies." *Reading Teacher* 61 (5): 364–373.

Allington, R. L. 2002. "What I've Learned About Effective Reading Instruction from a Decade of Studying Exemplary Elementary Classroom Teachers." *Phi Delta Kappan* 83 (10): 740–747.

———. 2005. "The Other Five 'Pillars' of Effective Reading Instruction." *Reading Today* 11 (6): 3.

———. 2006a. *What Really Matters for Struggling Readers: Designing Research-Based Programs*. 2nd ed. Boston: Allyn & Bacon.

———. 2006b. "Research and the Three-Tier Model." *Reading Today* 23 (5): 20.

———. 2008. *What Really Matters in Response to Intervention: Research-Based Designs*. Boston: Allyn & Bacon.

Allington, R. L., and P. H. Johnston. 2000. *What Do We Know About Effective Fourth-Grade Teachers and Their Classrooms?* Report Series 13010. Albany, NY: National Research Center on English Learning and Achievement.

———. 2002. *Reading to Learn: Lessons from Exemplary Fourth-Grade Classrooms*. New York: Guilford.

Allington, R. L., and S. A. Walmsley. 1995. *No Quick Fix: Rethinking Literacy Programs in America's Elementary Schools*. New York: Teachers College Press.

———. 2007. *No Quick Fix: Rethinking Literacy Programs in America's Elementary Schools*. The RTI Edition. New York: Teachers College Press.

Allison, N. 2007. *Supporting Independent Readers: Instructional Strategies to Improve Proficiency and Engagement*. Norwood, MA: Christopher-Gordon.

Ankrum, J. W., and R. M. Bean. 2007. "Differentiated Reading Instruction: What and How." *Reading Horizons* 48 (1): 133–146.

Atwell, N. 2007. *The Reading Zone: How to Help Kids Become Skilled, Passionate, Habitual, Critical Readers*. New York: Scholastic.

Bender, W. N., and C. Shores. 2007. *Response to Intervention: A Practical Guide for Every Teacher*. Thousand Oaks, CA: Corwin Press.

Bentum, K. E., and P. G. Aaron. 2003. "Does Reading Instruction in Learning Disability Resource Rooms Really Work? A Longitudinal Study." *Reading Psychology* 24 (3/4): 361–382.

Betts, E. A. 1946. *Foundations of Reading Instruction.* New York: American Book Co.

Brown-Chidsey, R., and M. W. Steege. 2005. *Response to Intervention: Principles and Strategies for Effective Practice.* New York: Guilford.

Caldwell, J. 2002. *Reading Assessment: A Primer for Teachers and Tutors.* New York: Guilford.

Cambourne, B., and J. Turbill. 1990. "Assessment in Whole Language Classrooms: Theory into Practice." *Elementary School Journal* 90 (3): 337–349.

Cassidy, J., and D. Cassidy. "What's Hot." *Reading Today.* Articles in issues 1996 to 2008.

Clay, M. 1985. *The Early Detection of Reading Difficulties.* Portsmouth NH: Heinemann.

———. 2006. *An Observation Survey of Early Literacy Achievement.* Revised 2nd ed. Portsmouth, NH: Heinemann.

Cooper, J. D., D. J. Chard, and N. D. Kiger. 2006. *The Struggling Reader: Interventions That Work.* New York: Scholastic.

Covey, S. R. 2004. *The 7 Habits of Highly Effective People.* 15th anniversary ed. New York: Free Press.

Cunningham, P. M., and R. L. Allington. 2006. *Classrooms That Work: They Can All Read and Write.* 4th ed. Boston: Allyn & Bacon.

Diller, D. 2007. *Making the Most of Small Groups: Differentiation for All.* Portland, ME: Stenhouse.

———. 2008. *Spaces and Places: Designing Classrooms for Literacy.* Portland, ME: Stenhouse.

Dorn, L., C. French, and T. Jones. 1998. *Apprenticeship in Literacy: Transitions Across Reading and Writing.* Portland, ME: Stenhouse.

Dorn, L. J., and C. Soffos. 2001. *Shaping Literate Minds: Developing Self-Regulated Learners.* Portland, ME: Stenhouse.

Duke, N. K. 2000. "3.6 Minutes per Day: The Scarcity of Informational Texts in First Grade." *Reading Research Quarterly* 35 (2): 202–224.

———. 2004. "The Case for Informational Text." *Educational Leadership* 61 (6): 40–44.

Edwards, P. A., J. D. Turner, and K. Mokhtari. 2008. "Balancing the Assessment *of* Learning and *for* Learning in Support of Student Literacy Achievement." *Reading Teacher* 61 (18): 682–684.

Farstrup, A. E. 2007. "RTI: A Vital Concern for Reading Professionals." *Reading Today* 25 (3): 17.

———. 2008. "A New School Year: Challenges and Opportunities." *Reading Today* 26 (2): 21.

Ferguson, A. 1992. "Communication: The Key to Reading Pull-Out Programs." *Ohio Reading Teacher* 26 (3): 6–8.

Fisher, D., and N. Frey. 2007. *Checking for Understanding: Formative Assessment Techniques for Your Classroom.* Alexandria, VA: ASCD.

———. 2008a. "Releasing Responsibility." *Educational Leadership* 66 (3): 32–37.

———. 2008b. *Better Learning Through Structured Teaching: A Framework for the Gradual Release of Responsibility.* Alexandria, VA: ASCD.

Fisher, D., N. Frey, and D. Lapp. 2008a. *In a Reading State of Mind: Brain Research, Teacher Modeling, and Comprehension Instruction.* Newark, DE: IRA.

———. 2008b. "Shared Readings: Modeling Comprehension, Vocabulary, Text Structures, and Text Features for Older Readers." *Reading Teacher* 61 (7): 548–556.

Gladwell, M. 2007. *Blink: The Power of Thinking Without Thinking.* Bel Air, CA: Back Bay Books.

Goodman, K. 1969. "Analysis of Oral Reading Miscues: Applied Psycholinguistics." In *Language and Literacy: The Selected Writings of Kenneth Goodman,* vol. 1, edited by F. Gollasch. Boston: Routledge and Kegan Paul.

Goodman, Y. 1978. "Kidwatching: Observing Children in the Classroom." In *Observing the Language Learner,* edited by A. Jagger and M. T. Smith-Burke. Newark, DE: IRA.

Gregory, G. H., and C. Chapman. 2006. *Differentiated Instructional Strategies: One Size Doesn't Fit All.* 2nd ed. Thousand Oaks, CA: Corwin Press.

Hall, S. L. 2008. *Implementing Response to Intervention: A Principal's Guide.* Thousand Oaks, CA: Corwin Press.

Hess, F. M. 2009. "The New Stupid." *Educational Leadership* 66 (4): 12–17.

Holdaway, D. 1979. *The Foundations of Literacy.* Sydney: Ashton Scholastic.

———. 1983. "Shared Book Experience: Teaching Reading Using Favorite Books." *Theory into Practice* 21 (4): 293–300.

Hoyt, L. 2005. *Spotlight on Comprehension: Building a Literacy of Thoughtfulness.* Portsmouth, NH: Heinemann.

Individuals with Disabilities Education Act. 2004. 108th Congress, H.R. 1350.

International Reading Association. 2000. "Making a Difference Means Making It Different: Honoring Children's Rights to Excellent Reading Instruction." A Position Statement of the International Reading Association. Newark, DE: International Reading Association.

International Reading Association and National Council of Teachers of English. 1994. *Standards for the Assessment of Reading and Writing.* Newark, DE: International Reading Association; Urbana IL: National Council of Teachers of English.

Johnston, P. H. 2004. *Choice Words: How Our Language Affects Children's Learning.* Portland, ME: Stenhouse.

———. 2005. "Assessment Conversations." In *Reading Assessment: Principles and Practices for Elementary Teachers,* 2nd ed., edited by S. J. Barrentine and S. M. Stokes. Newark, DE: International Reading Association.

Johnston, P. H., and P. Costello. 2005. "Principles for Literacy Assessment." *Reading Research Quarterly* 40 (2): 256–267.

Kopkowski, C. 2008. www.nea.org/neatoday/0804/whytheyleave.html.

Kotter, J. P. 2008. *A Sense of Urgency.* Boston, MA: Harvard Business Press.

Krashen, S. D. 2004. *The Power of Reading: Insights from the Research.* 2nd ed. Portsmouth, NH: Heinemann.

Lipson, M. Y., and K. K. Wixson. 2008. "New IRA Commission Will Address RTI Issues." *Reading Today* 26 (1): 1, 5.

Loflin, J., and T. Musig. 2007. *Juggling Elephants: An Easier Way to Get Your Most Important Things Done—Now!* New York: Portfolio (Penguin Group).

Manzo, K. K. 2008. "Federal Path for Reading Questioned: 'Reading First' Poor Results Offer Limited Guidance." *Education Week* 28 (14): 1, 16.

Mesmer, E. M., and H. A. E. Mesmer. 2009. "Response to Intervention (RTI): What Teachers of Reading Need to Know." *Reading Teacher* 62 (4): 280–290.

Meyer, C. A. 1992. "What's the Difference Between "Authentic" and "Performance" Assessment?" *Educational Leadership* 49 (8): 39–40.

Miller, D. 2002. *Reading with Meaning: Teaching Comprehension in the Primary Grades.* Portland, ME: Stenhouse.

———. 2008. *Teaching with Intention: Defining Beliefs, Aligning Practice, and Taking Action, K–5.* Portland, ME: Stenhouse.

Mokhtari, K., C. A. Rosemary, and P. A. Edwards. 2008. "Making Instructional Decisions Based on Data: What, How, and Why." *Reading Teacher* 61 (4): 354–359.

Muth, J. J. 2002. *The Three Questions.* New York: Scholastic.

National Association of State Directors of Special Education. 2008. *Response to Intervention: Blueprints for Implementation (School Building Level).* Alexandria, VA: National Association of State Directors of Special Education.

National Reading Panel. 2000. *Teaching Children to Read: An Evidence-Based Assessment of the Scientific Research Literacy on Reading and Its Implications for Reading Instruction.* Bethesda, MD: National Institute of Child Health and Human Development.

Noddings, N. 2008. "All Our Students Thinking." *Educational Leadership* 65 (5): 8–13.

O'Connor, R. E., K. M. Bell, K. R. Harty, et al. 2002. "Teaching Reading to Poor Readers in the Intermediate Grades: A Comparison of Text Difficulty." *Journal of Educational Psychology* 94 (3): 474–485.

Ohanian, S. 1999. *One Size Fits Few: The Folly of Educational Standards.* Portsmouth, NH: Heinemann.

Opitz, M. 2000. *Rhymes and Reasons: Literature and Language Play for Phonological Awareness.* Portsmouth, NH: Heinemann.

Pearson, P. D., and M. Gallagher. 1983. "The Instruction of Reading Comprehension." *Contemporary Educational Psychology* 8 (3): 317–344.

Pikulski, J. 2007. Review of *No Quick Fix.* http://search.barnesandnoble.com/No-Quick-Fix-the-RTI-Edition/Richard-L-Allington/e/9780807748442.

Powell, W. R., and C. G. Dunkeld. 1971. "Validity of the IRI Reading Levels." *Elementary English* 48 (6): 637–642.

Pressley, M., R. Wharton-McDonald, R. Allington, et al. 1998. *The Nature of Effective First-Grade Literacy Instruction.* Albany, NY: National Research Center on English Learning and Achievement.

Raphael, T. E. 1986. "Teaching Question-Answer Relationships, Revisited." *Reading Teacher* 39 (6): 516–522.

Raphael, T. E., K. Highfield, and K. H. Au. 2006. *QAR Now: A Powerful and Practical Framework That Develops Comprehension and Higher-Level Thinking in All Students.* New York: Scholastic.

Rasinski, T., W. H. Rupley, and W. D. Nichols. 2008. "Two Essential Ingredients: Phonics and Fluency Getting to Know Each Other." *Reading Teacher* 62 (3): 257–260.

Reilly, M. A. 2007. "Choice of Action: Using Data to Make Instructional Decisions in Kindergarten." *Reading Teacher* 60 (8): 770–776.

Robb, L. 2008. *Differentiating Reading Instruction: How to Teach Reading to Meet the Needs of Each Student.* New York: Scholastic.

Routman, R. 1991. *Invitations: Changing as Teachers and Learners K–12.* Portsmouth, NH: Heinemann.

———. 2002. "Teacher Talk." *Educational Leadership* 59 (6): 32–35.

———. 2003. *Reading Essentials: The Specifics You Need to Teach Reading Well.* Portsmouth, NH: Heinemann.

———. 2008. *Teaching Essentials: Expecting the Most and Getting the Best from Every Learner, K–8.* Portsmouth, NH: Heinemann.

Smith, F. 1987. *Joining the Literacy Club: Further Essays into Education.* Portsmouth, NH: Heinemann.

Stiggins, R. J. 2002. "Assessment Crisis: The Absence of Assessment FOR Learning." *Phi Delta Kappan* 83 (10): 758–765.

Taberski, S. 2000. *On Solid Ground: Strategies for Teaching Reading K–3.* Portsmouth, NH: Heinemann.

———. 2009. *It's ALL About Comprehension.* Portsmouth, NH: Heinemann.

Taylor, B. M., D. S. Peterson, P. D. Pearson, and M. C. Rodriguez. 2002. "Looking Inside Classrooms: Reflecting on the 'How' as Well as the 'What' in Effective Reading Instruction." *Reading Teacher* 56 (3): 270–79.

Tomlinson, C. A. 1999. *The Differentiated Classroom: Responding to the Needs of All Learners.* Alexandria, VA: ASCD.

———. 2001. *How to Differentiate Instruction in Mixed-Ability Classrooms.* 2nd ed. Alexandria, VA: ASCD.

———. 2008. "The Goals of Differentiation." *Educational Leadership* 66 (3): 26–30.

Tooms, A., N. Padak, and T. Rasinski. 2007. *The Principal's Essential Guide to Literacy in the Elementary School.* New York: Scholastic.

Valencia, S. W., and M. R. Buly. 2005. "Behind Test Scores: What Struggling Readers *Really* Need." In *Reading Assessment: Principles and Practices for Elementary Teachers,* 2nd ed., edited by Shelby J. Barrentine and Sandra M. Stokes. Newark, DE: International Reading Association.

Vygotsky, L. S. 1978. *Mind in Society: The Development of Higher Psychological Processes.* Cambridge, MA: Harvard University Press.

Wallis, J. 2009. "Strategies to Support Assessment in the Classroom: Using What We Do to Learn What Our Students Need." In *Reading on the Edge: Enabling, Empowering, and Engaging Middle School Readers,* edited by Leigh Van Horn. Norwood, MA: Christopher-Gordon.

Walpole, S., and K. L. Blamey. 2008. "Elementary Literacy Coaches: The Reality of Dual Roles." *Reading Teacher* 62 (3): 222–231.

Wiggins, G. 1992. "Reading Assessment: Time for a Change." *Reading Teacher* 43: 726–732.

Wiggins, G., and J. McTighe. 2006. *Understanding by Design.* 2nd ed. Upper Saddle River, NJ: ASCD.

Wong, S., L. Groth, and J. O'Flahavan. 1994. *Characterizing Teacher-Student Interaction in Reading Recovery Lessons.* Reading Research Report No. 17. College Park, MD: National Reading Research Center.

Wood, D., J. S. Bruner, and G. Ross. 1976. "The Role of Tutoring in Problem Solving." *Journal of Child Psychology and Psychiatry* 17 (2): 89–100.

Wormeli, R. 2006. *Fair Isn't Always Equal: Assessing and Grading in the Differentiated Classroom.* Portland, ME: Stenhouse.

INDEX

potential phase, RTI as being in, xiv

Powell, William R. ("Validity of the IRI Reading Levels"), 46

Principal's Essential Guide to Literacy in the Elementary School, The (Tooms, Padak and Rasinski), 73

progress monitoring, 104–8
  defined, 96, 104
  interpreting and monitoring, 107–8
  persons to conduct, selecting, 106–7
  problems with, 104–5
  scheduling, 105–6

pull-out interventions, 26–27, 81, 89
  for tier 2, 70

purpose, maintaining clear sense of, 115–16

push-in interventions, 26–27
  for tier 2, 70

Q

QAR (question-answer-relationship), 105

qualitative and quantitative data, placing equal emphasis on, 102

R

Rasinski, Timothy
  Principal's Essential Guide to Literacy in the Elementary School, The, 73
  "Two Essential Ingredients," 43

reading, as reciprocal with writing, 14

Reading Essentials (Routman), 48

Reading First
  problems with, 37
  research on, xv, 3

reading games, in tier 2 interventions, 74

reading levels, determining, in tier 1 interventions, 46–47

Reading Recovery
  determining reading levels, 46
  research on, 5
  "roaming in the known" phase of, 75

reading specialists, as teachers for tier 3 instruction, 80–81

Reading with Meaning (Miller), 42, 50

reading workshop, in tier 1 interventions, 36

Reilly, Mary Ann ("Choice of Action"), 94, 103

reinforcing, in tiers, 25

"Releasing Responsibility" (Fisher and Frey), 49

remediation
  defined, 73
  and intervention in tier 2 interventions, distinguishing between, 74–75

research
  in NRP report (*see Teaching Children to Read* (National Reading Panel))
  scientifically based, 7
  underpinnings of RTI, 3–4

research-based instruction, 7

resources
  at appropriate levels of challenge, in RTI, 18
  for implementing RTI, 113
  reviewing, 6–7

response to instruction, 21

"Response to Intervention (RTI)" (Mesmer and Mesmer), 62

response to interventions (RTI)
  basic premises, 28–29
  changing face of, 28–29
  clear descriptors with specific guidelines, need to establish, 12–15
  components, 13–14
  creation of, xiii, 4
  defined, 3
  features, 28–29
  implementation, key points for full-scale, 112–16
  as literacy framework, 14, 15–18
  materials produced for, problems with, xiv–xv, 5–7
  organizational structure (*see* organizational structure)
  in potential phase, xiv, 18
  principles, essential, 29–32
  research underpinnings of, 3–4
  resources, reviewing, 6–7

responsive teaching, 42

Rigby, 62

Robb, Laura (*Differentiating Reading Instruction*), 40

"Role of Tutoring in Problem Solving, The" (Wood, Bruner and Ross), 84

Ross, Gail ("Role of Tutoring in Problem Solving, The"), 84

Routman, Regie
Invitations: Changing as Teachers and Learners K–12, 50
Reading Essentials, 48, 116
Teaching Essentials, 103

RTI Action Network, 5, 22–23

Rupley, William H. ("Two Essential Ingredients"), 43

teaching. *See* instruction

Teaching Children to Read (National Reading Panel), 6, 7
  emphasis in, 4–5, 92
  formation of panel, 4
  ignoring of some research, 7–8, 13
  incorporated into NCLB and RTI, 4–5
  lack of teaching recommendations in, 12
  publications following, rapid out-pouring of, 4–5

Teaching Essentials (Routman), 103

teaching with a sense of urgency, 116

Teaching with Intention (Miller), 44

team decision making, in tier 2 interventions, 65–66

testing culture, 2

test prep mentality, 52

texts
  in determining reading levels, 46
  interesting, access to, 13–14
  matching pupils to, 13
  providing, that students can read, 30–31, 38
  in tier 1 interventions, 38–39, 51–52
  in tier 2 interventions, 74
  in tier 3 interventions, 85–86

Thoreau, Henry D., 78

Three Questions, The (Muth), 56

three-tiered model of RTI, 23–24

tier 1 interventions, 34–55
  assessment, 44–47
  components of effective instruction, 35–47
  curriculum, 37–40
  daily schedule, 36
  differentiated instruction, 40–42, 53–55
  high-quality, insuring, 51–52
  interactive relationship to tier 2, 59
  overview, 23–24, 34–35
  reading levels, determining, 46–47
  targeting instruction, 42–44
  teaching, framework for, 48–51

tier 2 interventions, 56–77
  assessment, 60–61, 64, 75
  collaboration, 65–66
  designing, 72–77
  effective instruction, 75

  features, 60–66
  flexibility as crucial element, 68, 76–77
  goal, 60
  instructional intensity, increasing, 71–72
  interactive relationship to tier 1, 59
  interventionists, deciding on, 68–69
  locations for, 70
  number of sessions, 71
  overview, 24, 59–61
  pie theory, 74–75
  students, examples of, 57–59, 66–68
  supplementary resources, 60, 61–63
  targeted interventions, 60, 63
  team decision making, 61, 65–66
  and tier 3 interventions, distinguishing between, 79–80
  value of, 57
  when and how often to provide, 68–69

tier 3 interventions, 78–90
  assessment, 81, 86–87, 88
  designing, 83–86
  flexibility as crucial element, 89–90
  interventionists, selecting, 80–81
  number of sessions, 82
  overview, 24, 79–80
  pie theory, 85
  and special education, relationship between, 81–82
  students, examples of, 82–83, 86–88
  and tier 2 interventions, distinguishing between, 79–80

tiers. *See also individual tiers*
  coordinated supports for, 114
  interconnected, instruction in tiers as, 24–25
  overview of, 22–25
  three-tiered model, 23–24

time
  as essential principle of RTI, 30
  luscious feeling of endless time, 44
  in tier 1 interventions, 51

Time for Kids, 67

Title 1, teachers for tier 3 instruction, 80–81

Tomlinson, Carol Ann
  Differentiated Classroom, The, 39
  "Goals of Differentiation, The," 40